BAAL SHEM TOV

RABBI YISRAEL BEN ELIEZER
THE LEGENDARY KABBALAH MASTER

KESER SHEM TOV

MYSTICAL TEACHINGS ON
THE TORAH

VOLUME I

By Rabbi Yehoshua Starrett

BST Publishing
Cleveland, Ohio

Translation and Commentary by Rabbi Yehoshua Starrett
Copyright © 2008 by BST Publishing
Printed in the United States of America

For information regarding permission to reprint material from this book, please e-mail your request to info@baalshemtov.com.

ISBN: 978-0-9853562-3-1

Library of Congress Control Number: 2012956448
Library of Congress subject heading:
1. Hasidim — Legends. 2. Baal Shem Tov, ca. 1700 - 1760 — Legends. 3. Hasidism. 4. Mysticism Judaism. 5. Title.

BST Publishing
Cleveland, OH 44124
info@ baalshemtov.com
www. baalshemtov.com

Dedicated to the millions of Chassidim and their Rebbes, who for nearly three centuries, have cherished and passed these holy teachings down to us.

 יברכך יי וישמרך
יאר יי פניו אליך ויחנך
ישא יי פניו אליך וישם לך שלום

"May the L•rd bless you and guard you. May the L•rd make His countenance shine upon you and be gracious to you. May the L•rd turn His countenance towards you and grant you peace."

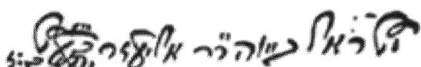

Yisrael Ben Moreinu Rabbeinu HaRav Rav Eliezer
KoesB (presently in) Medzibush
Signature of the Baal Shem Tov

TABLE OF CONTENTS

INTRODUCTION

And these are the holy words of the holy and awesome Rav, our teacher, the Baal Shem Tov of blessed memory for everlasting life in the world to come. These words "which were brought into the house of Yoseph" (books of Rav Yaakov Yoseph of Polonoye) were found in the holy books of his student – the Rav, the great Goan, the Chassid, our teacher, R. Yaakov Yosef of Polonoye, of blessed memory for everlasting life in the world to come, the head of the court of the holy community of Polonoye. The holy books [from where these teachings were collected] are the Sefer *Ben Poras Yoseph*, the Sefer *Toldos Yaakov Yosef* and the Sefer *Tnafnas Panach.*

And behold, the one who collected [these teachings] is the young man Aaron, the son of my teacher and Rav Tzvi Hirsch HaCohane from the holy community of Apta. I [Reb Aaron] collected all the holy words of the Baal Shem Tov from the

1

seforim (books) mentioned above and also from other short and lengthy discourses of the Rav, the Goan, R. Yaakov Yoseph (of blessed memory for everlasting life in the world to come). Other teachings of R. Yaakov Yoseph (not related to the Baal Shem Tov) were left out of this holy book. I only put in this Holy Book what relates to the holy words of the Baal Shem Tov. The whole world is full of the honor and the glory of his (the Baal Shem Tov's) kingdom and the beauty of his greatness. And the world is illuminated from his wisdom. Also, I collected the words of the Baal Shem Tov from other books of collected sayings and treasures that were printed. Note that in this book I did not write any explanation of the teachings of the holy Baal Shem Tov. They are written, however, in books that are found by me called – the sefer *Sanctify Shabbos* on the Tractate Shabbos, the sefer *Secrets Of Shabbos* on Tractate *Eruvin* and the sefer *Magen Avos*.

1. THE LETTER

To my beloved brother-in-law, my friend who is dear to me as my own heart and soul, the exalted rabbi and Chasid, renowned for his Torah scholarship and fear of Heaven, our master, Rabbi Avraham Gershon, may his light shine. Peace unto him and his family, his modest wife, Bluma, together with all their children; may they be blessed with life, amen, sela.

I received the letter written by your holy hand, which you sent by means of the emissary from Jerusalem, at the fair of Luka in the year 5510 (1750 c.e.). It was written with extreme brevity, explaining that you had already written at length to each of us individually and had sent those letters by means of a certain man en route to Egypt. However, the letters never arrived, and I was sorely grieved that I never saw the work of your holy hand which was written in greater detail. Assuredly this is due to the calamitous state of the many lands in which the plague has spread because of our many transgressions.   Not far from our region the pestilence has reached the holy community of Mohilev, as well as Wallachia and Turkey.

[Your letter] also states that the Torah teachings and mystical revelations which I sent you through the rabbi and preacher of the holy community of Polonoye did not reach you; this, too, caused me great distress. It certainly would have given you great joy if they had reached you. I have since forgotten many [of those teachings]. However, the few details I still remember I will write to you in brief.

On Rosh Hashanah of the year 5507 (1746 c.e.), I made a [Kabalistic] oath and elevated my soul in the manner known to you. I saw wondrous things in a vision, the likes of which I had never witnessed since the day my mind first began to awaken. The things that I saw and learned when I ascended there would be impossible to communicate, even if I could speak to you in person. When I returned to the lower Garden of Eden, I saw many souls, both living and dead, some known to me, and others unknown — their number was beyond reckoning. They were hastening to and fro in order to ascend from one world to another through the Column known to those initiated into the Mysteries. Their joy was too great for the mouth to express or the physical ear to hear. Also, many evildoers were repenting, and their sins were being forgiven, since it was a special time of Divine favor. Even to me, it was amazing how many of them were accepted as penitents, a number of whom you also know. There was great joy among them, too, and they ascended in the same manner.

Together, they begged and implored me unceasingly, "Because of the glory of your Torah, G•d has granted you an additional measure of understanding to grasp and to know these matters. Ascend with us so that you can be our help and support."

Because of the great joy that I beheld among them, I agreed to go up with them . . . And I besought my master (Achiyah HaShiloni) to accompany me, for the ascent to the Supernal Worlds is fraught with danger. From the day of my birth until now, I never experienced such an ascent as this.

I went up from level to level until I entered the Palace of Moshiach, where Moshiach studies with the sages and righteous, as well as with the Seven Shepherds. There I found extremely great rejoicing, but I did not know the cause of this delight. At first I thought that it might be due to my having passed away from the physical world, G•d forbid. Later, they told me that I had not yet died, for they have great pleasure on high when I effect mystical unifications in the world below through their holy Torah. However, to this very day, the nature of their joy remains unknown to me.

I asked Moshiach, "When will you come, Master?" And he replied, "By this you shall know: it will be a time when your teachings become publicized and revealed to the world, and your wellsprings have overflowed to the outside. [It will be when] that which I have taught you — and that which you have perceived of your own efforts — become known, so that others, too, will be able to perform mystical unifications and ascents of the soul like you. Then all the evil klipot (forces) will be destroyed, and it will be a time of grace and salvation."

I was amazed at this and greatly troubled, since a long time must pass for this to be possible. But while I was there, I learned three segulot and three Holy Names that are easy to learn and explain. My mind was then set at ease, and I thought that with these teachings the people of my own generation might attain the same spiritual level and state as myself. They would be able to elevate their souls and to learn and perceive just as I do. However, I was not granted permission to reveal this during my lifetime. I pleaded for your sake to be allowed to teach you; but I was denied permission altogether and took an oath to that effect.

Yet this I can tell you, and may G•d assist you, so that your way be pleasant to the L•rd: Never stray, particularly in the Holy Land, whenever you pray or study, and with every utterance of your lips, from intending to bring about the unification of a Divine Name, for every letter contains worlds and souls and G•dliness, and they ascend and combine and unite with one another. Then the letters combine and unite to form a word, and they are actually unified with the Divine essence — and in all these aspects, your soul is bound up with them. All the worlds become unified as one, and they ascend and bring about great joy and delight without measure. Consider the joy of a bridegroom and bride in this lowly physical world, and you will realize how much greater is the joy on such a lofty spiritual level.

G•d will surely help you. Wherever you turn, you will succeed and become enlightened. "Give wisdom to the wise, and he will become wise all the more." The Keser Shem Tov version ends here.

Please pray for my sake, that I might be privileged to dwell in G•d's land during my lifetime; and pray for the remnant of our people who still remain in the Diaspora.

These are the words of your brother-in-law who longs to see you face-to-face, who prays that length of days be granted to you and your wife and children, and who wishes you peace "all your days — including the nights, for many good years, amen, sela.

Israel Baal Shem Tov
of the Holy Community of Medzhibush

3. The Baal Shem Tov discusses the futility of man's effort to know the unknowable — and how he may find spiritual growth and satisfaction in the process of discovery — not in the discovery itself:

The Baal Shem Tov discusses the following phrase in the Talmud:

"If only they had abandoned Me but kept My Torah."[1]

The ultimate goal in striving to know G•d is the understanding that one truly cannot know G•d. [And man thus remains ignorant of this

---

[1] Medrash

8

understanding]. However, there are two categories of such "ignorance".

The first category is that of a person who immediately realizes their limitations. Since they understand that it is impossible to truly know (G•d), they abandon any further effort to contemplate the matter.

The second category is that of a person who also immediately realizes their limitations. Nevertheless, they continue their effort to search until they know that it is truly impossible to know (G•d).

The difference between these two categories can be explained with the following parable.

Two of the king's subjects want to know the king.

The first person walks through the king's palace observing the wealth and luxury of the king. He delights in all he sees, yet he realizes that despite all that he sees, he doesn't truly know the king — he is only seeing the king's possession.

We can thus better understand the two categories mentioned above.

One individual makes an effort to know the king and does not succeed, while the other does not even attempt to try, and also doesn't succeed.

So when G•d says, "They abandon Me", it refers to the "avodah" [spiritual effort] in trying to know G•d. Nevertheless, says G•d, "If only they had abandoned Me", knowing that they can not ultimately know Me. But the "abandoning" only occurred after they engaged in the process of searching until "they had kept my Torah" (and had explored all its depth). *Yerushalmi, Chagigah* 1:7 (6b)

4. The Baal Shem Tov taught:

Every individual must live and conduct himself according to standards of his own spiritual level. However, when one tries to conduct his life by the standards of someone else's spiritual level, he will fail by both standards. This is the deeper meaning of the sages' teaching, "Many tried to emulate Rabbi Shimon bar Yochai, but they were unsuccessful."[2] This means that though they themselves were not on Rabbi Shimon's spiritual level, they tried to live according the high standard by which they saw him living, and that is why they were unsuccessful.[3]

---

[2] Tractate *Brachot* 35b

[3] The underlying thought of this teaching is that every person must be true to himself and live his own truth within the

Furthermore, the sages teach us that Truth is G•d's seal (*Genesis Rabbah* 81:2), and truth is the only gateway to G•d (*Likkutei Moharan I* 9:3). If one is not living truthfully with oneself, one cannot be living with G•d. And finally, since no one can truly grasp the spiritual level of another person, following the unique behavior of another person can be nothing more than mimicking his conduct, and is doomed to failure, as the Baal Shem Tov says here.

5. The Baal Shem Tov taught:

"A bat kol (a voice from Heaven) comes out from Mount Chorev (Mount Sinai) and says, "The entire world is sustained b'shvil (literally, for the sake of) my son Chanina . . . . " Tractate *Berochot* 17b. The Hebrew word "shvil" also means a path, a channel. Thus, the sages mean here that Rabbi Chanina opened up a channel and a path for the flow of Divine beneficence, and hence, "The entire world is sustained through the shvil of my son Chanina".[4]

---

framework of the Torah. Every person was brought into this world for a very specific purpose, and if one tries be someone else, one has betrayed his own soul (*Toldot Yaakov Yoseph, VaYishlach* #8, *Metzora* #1).

[4] This teaching is based on the premise that there can be no interaction between two utterly different states of existence,

6. From the Baal Shem Tov comes an explanation of the following phrase from the Gemorah. [Our sages teach us that "a bas kol (voice from Heaven) comes out from Mount Chorev and says the entire world is sustained b'shvil (for the sake of) my son Chanina . . . " Tractate *Brochot* 17b. [The word shvil also means path.] For shvil is a channel, and [Chanina] opened up a channel and a path for the spiritual flow. And this is what it says "G•d said, through the shvil of my son Chanina."

"And the thing which is too hard come to me." (Devarim 1:17) The Baal Shem Tov explained in the name of the Ramban (Nachmanides) that he

---

specifically, between the spiritual and material worlds, without a medium, an intermediary state, an entity that has aspects of both (*Etz Chaim*, 42:1:42; *Toldot Yaakov Yoseph*, *Kedoshim* 5). Thus, we are taught that Moses served as the intermediary between G•d and man in transmitting the Torah, since Moses was, "the man of G•d" – he was G•dly, yet he was fully a man (Deuteronomy 33:1; *Sidduro Shel Shabbath*, II:2). In this regard, every tzaddik bears a spark of the "Moses soul," and is thus an intermediary – a *channel* – between G•d and man (*Meor Eynayim*, *VayeLech* [end]; *ibid. Yithro, q.v.* Tractate *Shabbat*). But this channel is not only for material benefits, but for spiritual ones as well. For example, the great tzaddikim pave new spiritual paths that are then open for others to travel, or sometimes just by their very attaining of spiritual heights, they make it easier for others to attain them with considerably less effort (*Noam ElimeLech*, *Chaya Sarah*, *q.v. V'Avraham Zaken*).

commanded to his son if you are doubtful in something whether to do it or not.

"If any case is too difficult for you, bring it to me . . ." (Deuteronomy 1:17)

The Baal Shem Tov taught in the name of the Ramban, who advised his son the following:

"Whenever there are various possible options of how to go about doing something, and you are in doubt as to which is the best way, or if you are in doubt whether or not doing it is at all G•d's will, in which case it should be done, or it is against His will, in which case it should not, you must first unattach yourself from all personal gain or honor you might derive from this action, and only then can you objectively weigh the options, for anything from which one derives any personal gain, one will search to find some way to permit even the forbidden. But after doing as said, G•d will guide you to the truth and you can feel secure that you are doing the right thing."

This then, is the meaning of the verse, "If any case is too difficult for you," that is, you don't know how or whether at all to do something, the doubt arises from *you* — from the personal gain that you would derive from doing it. Therefore, dis-attach yourself from the personal gain you would derive from doing it, and "bring it to *Me*" — that is, intend to do it for the sake of Heaven, without any motive for personal gain. Then [as the verse concludes], "I will hear it:" I will *make it heard* — I will give that person the understanding how to behave.[5]

7. From the Baal Shem Tov comes an explanation of the verse from Mishlei, "His woman [steered] his heart."

[Our sages teach us that] there is no word in the Torah that can't be understood in two ways. There are at least two categories of male and female. Being that this is the case, there is nothing that was created in this world that does not include

---

[5] The Baal Shem Tov adds to the Ramban's teaching that all doubts and difficulties we confront in life arise from our being out of touch with G•d and with our deepest selves. Instead, we live superficially, from momentary and ephemeral physical pleasure to the next momentary and ephemeral emotional gain, completely out of touch with what our souls deeply crave and need. We are thus torn in different directions at once, for we all have conflicting desires and interests. Only when we are able to see through those pleasures and gains, and touch with our deepest needs and with G•d, are we able to act assuredly from a place of Truth (*Sfat Emet*, Deuteronomy; *Likutim, Lech Lecha*)

something from the rest of creation. And the choice is given to him to sway towards some category that he wants. Thus, being that there are always at least two possible directions that we can travel, the woman is able to sway his heart.

13. "The spirit of G•d hovered above the surface of the water."[6]

"The spirit of G•d," refers to the human soul,[7] which must hover over "the surface of the water," which refers to the Torah.[8] Then, "G•d said, 'There shall be light,'"[9] which means that G•d will then enlighten the person with the holy Light of the Torah.

_____

[6] Genesis 1:2

[7] The *Midrash* says that this phrase refers to the spirit of the Adam and to the spirit of Moshiach (*Yalkut Shimoni*, Genesis #4). Actually, Adam, the first man, encompassed all mankind, and his name is seen as the acronym of A(dam), D(avid), M(oshiach). The Baal Shem Tov is adding here that this teaching, which is based on the verse that speaks about the purpose of Creation – "Let there be light" – is relevant to each and every one of us. Each of us can bring more light into our own lives, and automatically into the world, and be part of the "Moshiach," by connecting to G•d through His Torah.

[8] Tractate *Baba Kama* 17a

[9] Genesis 1:3

14. "Around midnight . . . "[10]

Doubt can be compared to midnight, [which is the exact point of time separating the first half of the night from the second. By the same token, when a person is in doubt, he sees opportunities and options] in both directions. Then, "I [G•d] will go out in the midst of Egypt,"[11] in the midst of that person's difficulties to enlighten him.[12]

16. "I see G•d from my flesh."[13]

The Baal Shem Tov taught:

Just as with physical relations, one cannot father a child without a "live" organ, which requires passion and joy, so with spiritual "relations," that is, the words of Torah and prayer,[14] one can only be

---

[10] Exodus 11:4
[11] *ibid.*
[12] This teaching is actually from the *Toldot Yaakov Yoseph* (*Mishpatim* 12). He says that when a person wants to make sure that what he is considering doing is indeed G•d's Will, he should arouse doubt in his mind by contemplating doing the exact opposite, and weigh up the two options equally and objectively. By so doing, G•d will enlighten him as to which is indeed His Will.
[13] Job 19:26
[14] Which is how one relates to G•d.

spiritually productive if one has a "live" organ, that is, if one experiences joy and pleasure.[15]

22. "One who learns one chapter of Torah from his companion, or one law, one verse, one phrase, or even just one letter, is obligated to treat him with honor, as we find that King David learned only two things from Achitophel, and he called him, 'My teacher, my mentor who enlightens me.' Thus, if King David gave Achitophel this honor for just teaching him two things, all the more so is the one who learns a chapter, a law, a verse, a phrase, or even just a letter from his companion obligated to treat him with honor."[16]

The Baal Shem Tov taught:

This Mishnah is difficult to understand. Firstly, what does it mean by, "only two things"? Secondly, whatever it means, the teaching derived from that instance cannot be more extreme than

---

[15] The point here is that it is not enough to study and pray with serious devotion, but that one must truly enjoy doing these things. The vivid metaphor implies that one's entire body must be enthusiastically involved in the practice, and not just the mind.

[16] Tractate *Avoth* 6:3

that instance itself, [and how can we learn from here even "one law", or "one letter"?

The answer is that whatever one learns from a fitting Torah teacher, that teaching will bear further fruit within the student. But whatever one learns from a wicked person will not bear fruit, but will remain within the student the same as when he learned it.[17]

Thus, if King David learned from the wicked Achitophel only two things – because they bore no fruit and remained only two things, as he had learned them from him – yet King David called him his teacher. When one who learns from his companion, that is a righteous person, in which case the Torah transmitted will bear fruit, he is certainly obligated to treat him with honor.

This also explains why the sages taught Torah "in the company" of Torah,[18] [so that the Torah being transmitted would multiply within the students].

25. The Baal Shem Tov taught:

When a person becomes aware of what deeply ails him, of the fact that he is spiritually ill, .i.e,

---

[17] *Toldot Yaakov Yoseph*, addendum #19 - 20
[18] Tractate *Brachot* 63b

that his mind is constricted in katnut/immature consciousness, this very awareness softens his constriction, and this awareness itself is the healing of his illness.[19]

However, if one is unaware — referred to as hester/concealed consciousness (as the verse says, "I will conceal Myself" (Deuteronomy 31:18) — and does not realize that he is spiritually ill, then there is nothing that can heal his wounds.

26. The Baal Shem Tov taught:

Since the Shechinah (the Divine Presence) encompasses all worlds — the inanimate, the plant, the animal, and the human worlds — including all

---

[19] The workings of person's soul are very deep and convoluted, and most people are not aware at all of what motivates them and why they act in certain ways. These motivations are usually based on deep seated emotional needs that were formed in one's early years, in one's "*katnut,*" one's childhood/adolescence. Because one's consciousness if constricted and limited during these years, these dynamics develop without one's awareness, and sink deeply into the unconsciousness. It may only be many years later that one begins to become aware of these deep seated motivations, and of how so much of his behavior arises from this immature consciousness. The Baal Shem Tov teaches us here that simply becoming more and more aware of these dynamics softens their grip on us, and gradually releases us from our constricted behavior patterns, revealing to us depths of soul that had previously been concealed. There is no other way to healing oneself, as the Baal Shem Tov concludes.

types of creatures, good and evil alike, and the Shechinah is the Absolute Unity, how can two utterly opposite entities exist in one thing? For good and evil are complete antitheses to each other, while the Shechinah is an Undifferentiated One.

However, evil is actually a vehicle of good. An example is when Pharaoh pursued the Jews to the Red Sea, regarding which the verse says that, "Pharaoh came close. . . ."[20] — literally, brought them close.[21] Another example is when one sees how the wicked behave, and then is grateful that one is not that way, in which case, the evil brings him the pleasure and satisfaction of being righteous. In fact, evil is virtually elevated in this way, only that as soon as the evil is thus elevated,

---

[20] Exodus 14:10

[21] By causing the Israelites to fear for their lives and to cry to G•d, Pharaoh was thus responsible for bringing them closer to G•d.

its evilness is dissipated.[22] An evil thought is also a vehicle in this fashion.[23]

Also, sometimes a soul descends from the world of Atzilut [the one closest to G•d] into the world of Asiyah [representing the physical world] and sees how people are not respecting the honor of the King of world. This soul is greatly distressed by this lack of respect for the King's honor, but then he has pleasure that he is not among those people.

This explains the verse, "G•d said to Abram"[24] (Abram symbolizes the soul, as stated in the Zohar[25]), "Go away from your homeland," that is, from the world of Atzilut to the world of Beriah [the world immediately below Atzilut], "and from your birthplace," that is, from the world of Beriah to the world of Yetzirah [the world below Beriah], "and from your father's house," that is, from Yetzirah to

---

[22] *Toldot Yaakov Yoseph, Lech Lecha* 1. This teaching can be understood within the context of the teaching that everything that G•d created is good – including the evil inclination (*Midrash*), and the existence of evil in this world is actually only from our perspective. Hence, when one reaches this realization, and uses "evil" for its true purpose of being a vehicle in various ways for reaching G•d, its evilness dissipates.

[23] That is, if one realizes that the thought was only sent to him for the purpose of his realizing that it was sent from G•d, this very realization brings him closer to G•d.

[24] Genesis 2:1

[25] 80b

Asiyah, which is, "the land that I will show you." That is, there you will see how the people of the world of Asiyah disrespect G•d's honor, and you should rebuke them.

27. "There was a famine in the land."[26]

This means that the people lacked faith in G•d,[27] that is, they were lax in honoring Him. Therefore, "Abram went down to Mitzrayim/ Egypt,"[28] which means that Abraham was distressed [mitzta'er] by this laxity in honoring G•d in the World of Action. However, as a result, "Abram went up from Mitzrayim,"[29] which means that he became spiritually elevated and was able to derive even greater pleasure from serving G•d, by virtue of the fact that he was not like them, since light can only be discerned in contrast to darkness.

Therefore, "Lot — who symbolizes the evil inclination — was with him,"[30] because the existence of evil allows one to derive even greater

---

26 Genesis 12:10. This piece is a continuation of the idea presented in #26.
27 *Zohar* I 80a
28 Genesis *ibid.*
29 Genesis 13:1
30 *Ibid.*

22

pleasure from serving G•d,[31] and evil thus become a vehicle to good, and becomes encompassed in it.

"And Abram was heavily laden with cattle, silver and gold,"[32] which means that he was able to extract the sparks of holiness, similarly to, "Joseph collected all the money in Egypt."[33]

29. "And now, Israel, what does G•d ask of you — only to have awe of G•d your L•rd."[34]

That is, G•d asks "what" of you — "what" implies humility and selflessness. When a person reaches this level, awe of G•d will be easily

---

[31] Thus, uprooting one's evil tendencies is not only anyway impossible, but also not the goal. On the contrary, one should rejoice that one has an evil tendency to deal with on a daily basis, and even enjoy the challenges it presents. This is how we grow spiritually, and every success brings us closer to G•d.
[32] *Ibid.* v. 2
[33] Genesis 47:14; *Degel Machneh Ephraim, ad loc.* This explains how evil itself becomes encompassed in the good. The Hebrew word for silver/money is *kesef*, which is the same root as desire. Thus, by seeing how mankind is so sunken in all sorts of desires, or when an undesirable desire rises one's own mind, one can turn this around and perceive it in this way: If the pleasure for this earthly thing is so great, how much greater is the pleasure of being with G•d, the Source and Creator of all pleasures. This can bring one to an intense experience of pleasure from being in G•d's presence. Then, those desires of others or oneself, which are actually fallen sparks of holiness, fallen and misguided desires for G•d, are elevated back to their Source.
[34] Deuteronomy 10:12

attainable for him, just as it was for Moses, as the verse concludes, "only to have awe."[35]

With this we can understand the verse, "His concubine,"[36] which refers to false humility, "whose name was Re'umah" — that is, re'u mah, which means, see that I am "what," that I possess humility. "[Re'umah] gave birth to Tevach" [tevach literally means slaughter], since this will eventually kill the person's soul.[37]

Similarly, the names of the Tribes, Reuben, Shimon, Levi, Judah, which have holy connotations, can also have unholy ones. For instance, Re'u ben — which means, see that I am a son (of G•d); Shim'on — which means, his fame, that is, one who acts properly so that fame becomes universally known; Levi Judah — which means accompaniment and praise, that is, one who accompanies the righteous so that he receive praise.

---

[35] As we saw in #29, the level of a person's awareness and experience of G•d is intimately connected with the level of his selflessness.
[36] The verse quoted in this paragraph is from Genesis 22:24.
[37] G•d, is the Source of all life and of Truth, and thus, any type of falseness inevitably dissociates one from G•d and leads to spiritual death.

32. "ואבוא היום אל העין – Today I arrived at the well."[38]
The Baal Shem Tov taught:

The Divine Name connected with translocation is found in the acronym of these words.[39]

"If she was speaking with someone in the market . . . ."[40]

The Baal Shem Tov taught:

This teaching can be understood with another one: "The one who reviews his lessons one hundred times is not comparable to the one who reviews his lessons one hundred and one times,"[41] that is, one hundred times with One — with G•d. Hence, a person must be able to remain with One — with G•d — even when one is speaking mundane

---

[38] Genesis 24:42

[39] The Hebrew letters, א ה ו ה, are connected with G•d because these same letters form the acronym of the words, את השמים ואת הארץ, referring to G•d's creating the heavens and the earth. This alludes to the singular Force that connects the earth with the heavens, meaning that the Supernal Light is evident even in the darkness on earth. From G•d's perspective, this is of course always true, but in order for it to be true from our perspective, this truth must be a vivid reality in one's life. When this is so, one is close to G•d, and as such, is not limited by the normal constrictions of time and space (*Sod Yesharim* II 72b).

[40] Tractate *Ketuboth* 13:1

[41] Tractate *Chagigah* 9b

conversation in the market: he must be able to see G•d in that conversation.[42]

33. "A person should always be accustomed to say, 'Everything that G•d does is for the best',"[43] as did Rabbi Akiba, whereas Nachum Ish Gamzu would always say, "This too is for the good."[44]

The Baal Shem Tov taught:

Nachum said, "This too is for the good," because he was able to actually transform the strict judgments at their source by finding some purposeful kindness in those specific judgments, and then everything was immediately transformed to an act of Divine kindness. The average person, though, who is unable to find the Divine kindness hidden in the source of judgment, should nevertheless always be accustomed to say in general, "Everything that G•d does is for the best,"

---

[42] This teaching was probably placed together with the previous one because the verse, "Today I arrived at the well," which contains an allusion to the Divine Name and to what was said in mundane conversation, thus meaning that it was expressed while maintaining G•d - consciousness.
[43] Tractate *Berachot* 60b
[44] Tractate *Taanit* 21a

even though he does not understand how this is true.

34. "Sometimes, violation of Torah is its observance. We learn this from G•d's telling Moses after his breaking the Tablets, 'That you broke,'[45] which implies approval for his having broken them."[46]

The Baal Shem Tov taught:

How can violating the Torah possibly enhance its observance? This can understood with the fact that all things yearn to return to their source. Therefore, when one eats, drinks, or is otherwise involved in mundane affairs, he is "violating" the Torah by his not studying it or explicitly serving G•d at that time. His soul then has a chance to rest from its enthusiasm, and it gathers new strength to return to an even higher level of closeness to G•d. This spiritual phenomenon is alluded to in the verse, "The chayot/angels run to

---

[45] Exodus 34:1
[46] Tractate *Menachot* 99b

and fro,"[47] and this is why "violating" the Torah sometimes is its observance.[48]

35. "Once, the king of beasts, the lion, became enraged with his subjects. The subjects gathered together to decide how to appease him, and the fox said that he would lead them to the lion, since he knew three hundred parables with which to assuage his feelings. They all followed, and little by little, the fox said that he had forgotten a portion of his parables, and by the time they reached the lion, he said that he had forgotten everything. Therefore, he said, each one should approach the king and appease him to the best of his abilities."

The fox's intention from the beginning, though, was only that they all follow him and

---

[47] Ezekiel 1:14

[48] *Toldot Yaakov Yoseph, Tazria* 2; Devarim 2. There are two reasons why this must be so. Firstly, if one were not to periodically "cool down" from intense spiritual experiences, one might reach a stage whereat one's soul would become so united with G•d that it would completely lose its separateness, at which point it would not be able to return to the physical body. Another reason is because perpetual pleasure loses its glamour, and becomes boredom. Thus, if one were constantly experiencing peak spiritual pleasures, they would no longer be pleasurable experiences. And regarding why one then rises to even more intense experiences, this is because the anguish of separation intensifies the pleasure of return.

surrender to the king, which is why he initially claimed what he did.

Similarly, the Baal Shem Tov urged people not to rely on the prayers of the prayer leaders on the Days of Awe, but that each individual should pray for himself.[49]

37. The Baal Shem Tov taught:

The purpose of light hearted conversation before Torah study is because human consciousness vacillates between a constricted state of mind, called "katnut [immature] ha'mochin," and an expanded state of mind, called "gadlut [mature] ha'mochin." These different states of mind are alluded to in the verse, "The chayot/angels run to and fro."[50] In order to rise

---

[49] This Midrash and the idea presented here are found in the *Ma'or Va'Shemesh* (*Shemini; Va'YeLech*), although not explicitly in the Baal Shem Tov's name. He presents it as relating to the tzaddik, who urges people to follow him to G•d, but them tells the m that the main thing is their own effort.
[50] Ezekiel 1:14. This means that the angels are in constant fluctuation between proximity to, and distance from G•d, and this is mirrored in the fluctuation of human consciousness, as said here. The need for this fluctuation is so that the created being be able to maintain its sense of existence as seemingly separate from G•d, for if it were to come to the absolute realization and experience that it in reality, it is non-existent outside of G•d, it would indeed lose this seemingly

from a constricted state of "immaturity" to an expanded state of "maturity," one can make use of light hearted jesting, thus opening his mind to learning and coming closer to G•d.[51]

Hence, the Talmud[52] tells of two saintly men who would jest with people in order to alleviate their suffering, after which there was a coming together of hearts, and they were able to elevate them.[53]

This is also alluded to in the verse, "[Abraham] took his two youths with him, and his

---

"independent" existence and be swallowed by the Divine Existence.

This spiritual phenomenon is mirrored in the waning and waxing in the physical world, as is evident from the moon's cycles, the waves of the ocean, and all the inherent cycles that we find at all levels in the natural world.

[51] Rebbe Nachman speaks profusely about how joy opens the mind and frees it of the bonds and constrictions of the normal states of consciousness, proclaiming, "It is a great mitzvah to always be happy!" (LM I 89; 222; 282; II 10; 24). Indeed, modern research has verified that a happy state of mind has very positive effects on the brain and hence on the entire body. But the point made here is to use this positive and expansive state of body/mind to come closer to G•d. On a deeper level, this very state of being is itself a proximity to G•d, as is for that matter any type of pleasure, since it is G•d's intention to provide us with pleasure, and all pleasures are in fact a constriction of Himself, so to speak, the Source of all pleasures.

[52] Tractate *Ta'anit* 22a

[53] *Toldot Yaakov Yoseph, Behar* #13.

30

son, Isaac," for by using jest[54] with holy intentions, one is able to elevate the years[55] of one's youth[56] with him as well.

38. The Baal Shem Tov taught:

Any fear of something in the external world that rises in a person's heart is actually G•d's right arm outstretched to rouse him to an existential fear [of G•d].[57] Thus, when a person becomes aware that this fearful experience is really G•d's kindness meant to rouse him, as said, this fear is transformed into love, because one then accepts it with love, and one is thus released from that fear.

---

[54] As known, Isaac's name comes from the root of laughing, and indeed, his mother Sarah gave him this name with that intention – "Whoever hears [that I gave birth at such an advanced age] will laugh" (Genesis 12:6).

[55] The Hebrew word for two can also mean years.

[56] "Youth" here refers to one's immature consciousness.

[57] In the text, and in general, these fears are respectively called, *Yir'ah Chitzonit*, and *Yir'ah Pnimit*, literally, an external or superficial fear and an internal fear, alluding to the teaching relayed here that the two are indeed just two levels of the same thing. In fact, the experience of fear itself is one and the same, and the difference is only how *we* perceive it. Do we become afraid of the superficial appearance that merely enclothes the Divine presence, or do we behold the Divine presence Itself, and stand in awe in front of It? (see *Toldot Yaakov Yoseph* #5; *Degel Machaneh Ephraim*, *VaYishlach*, *Ki Yareh*).

For the fear [of G•d] permeates all creatures and all worlds,[58] and the underlying source of all fears is the deep, inner, existential fear of G•d. Thus, even the fear of something external in the material world that rises in a person's heart is meant to rouse him to the fear of G•d. This is G•d's kindness, His right arm outstretched and begging man to become aroused to fear Him, as referred to in the verse, "What does G•d ask of you besides fearing G•d."[59]

And if a person would be aware of G•d's kindness and love towards him, in His sending him this fear of something external so that he become roused to an inner fear of G•d, then his fear is transformed into love, since he accepts the fear with complete love, and he is released from the fear.

---

[58] Fear for one's life — and all fear is a response to a situation perceived as a danger to one's life in some way — is actually something very existential to all living creatures, as is readily evidenced in the lower forms of life, and this fear is related to the survival instinct. However, on a deeper level, this existential fear can be traced back to the fact that ultimately, all creatures draw their lives from G•d at every single moment. Hence, since G•d can withdraw this life force at any given moment, it is only natural that at a very deep and unconscious level, all creatures have an existential fear of survival, knowing that G•d can indeed withdraw the spirit of life within them, and hence, this fear is actually a fear of G•d (see *Degel Machaneh Ephraim, Korach,* q.v. *Va'ani, Balak,* q.v. *V'yesh*).

[59] Deuteronomy 10:12

However, if one's sole intention is to become released from the fear, then this will not happen.[60]

And this is the meaning of the teaching, "Vis - à - vis Moses, fear is a minor thing,"[61] that is, from fear of a sage it is easy to reach fear of G•d.[62]

39. Rabbi Ze'ira said, "Whoever repeats the Shema Yisrael should be silenced."

Rabbi Papa asked Abaye, "Perhaps this person simply did not concentrate well the first time, and the second time he is able to concentrate."

"Does G•d have any friends in heaven? If he is unable to concentrate the first time," he answered him, "He is struck with a sledgehammer until he is able to concentrate."[63]

The Baal Shem Tov taught:

---

[60] As with everything, an ulterior motive does not achieve its goal. Here too, one must completely surrender to the fear and accept it as G•d's love, and only then is it transformed, but if one is trying to be released from the fear, one has not surrendered to it.

[61] Tractate *Berachot* 32b

[62] That is, while surrendering to the fear of a fearful situation in real life is not always easy, surrendering to the fear and awe that one has of a great sage and holy man is much easier, and it is that much easier to see G•d through him.

[63] Tractate *Berachot* 33a,34b

The question still remains, perhaps this person wants to repeat the verse because he was unable to concentrate the first time, and now he wants to fulfill his obligation and recite it with concentration. Furthermore, why does Rabbi Ze'ira only speak about someone who repeated the Shema Yisrael, and not about any other verse in the Keriat Shema, or any other verse, for that matter?

This can be understood by understanding what it means to accept the yoke of heaven. A person should believe that G•d's glory fills all worlds, and that there is nothing in which He does not exist. Thus, G•d's existence is inherent in all of man's thoughts, and each and every human thought is a complete spiritual structure on its own. Hence, when an untoward thought arises in one's mind during prayer, it arises so that he rectifies it and raises it back to its Source. If one does not believe this, then one has not fully accepted the yoke of heaven, for he is placing a limit on G•d's existence.

Thus, the person who repeated the Keriat Shema was because he had an untoward thought the first time. But had he known that even in that untoward thought he could have found G•d, he would not have had to repeat the verse. And this is what the Talmud alludes to by being struck with a sledgehammer;[64] the thoughts themselves are striking the person like a sledgehammer so that he rectify them and elevate them, so why does he have to repeat the Shema, which implies that G•d could not be found in his first recitation. By doing so, he places a limit on G•d's existence, and in the acceptance of the yoke of heaven, which is why he must be silenced.[65]

However, sometimes there are thoughts that one must push aside. The question is, then, how is one to know which to push aside and which to elevate? The answer to that is that one should take note if when the untoward thought arises in one's mind, if a corresponding thought of how to rectify and elevate it arises simultaneously in one's mind, then one should work with that thought to elevate it. However, if the thought of rectifying and elevating the untoward thought does not arise in one's mind, then the untoward thought was

---

[64] The usual understanding of this phrase in the Talmud is that he *should* be struck with a sledgehammer, but the Baal Shem Tov explains it to be saying that he is *being* struck by a sledgehammer.

[65] In this context, the opening exclamation, "Does G•d have friends in heaven?" means that if one could say that G•d is not alone in heaven, then one could argue that He is not everywhere, since He has to "share" the world with other beings, but since this is not so, then He must be everywhere, as the Baal She m Tov says here.

probably sent to him simply to confuse him and distract him from his prayers. In that case, one may push the thought aside, following the rule, "If someone is pursuing you to kill you, you may kill him first."[66]

In conclusion, if one has recited several words of the Shema or the prayers without proper concentration, one should not repeat those words orally, but one may think those words in his mind.[67]

43. "It was said that whenever Rabbi Yonathan son of Uziel sat down to delve into the Torah, any bird straying over his head was burnt by

---

[66] Tractate *Berachot* 58a

[67] This entire section is from the *Ben Porath Yoseph* 50b, c. The *Avodat Yisrael* (at the end of *Terumah*) also quotes the idea, but with a nuance of meaning. He says that the reason *why* the untoward thought arose in the person's mind was *because* he was anyway not concentrating properly.

Although some Chassidic texts warn against working with untoward thoughts in this way, saying that only tzaddikim should tackle this advanced spiritual practice, because one can easily get caught up in and carried away by the actual untoward thought, this warning may not apply if all one does is only acknowledges the presence of the thought, attributes it to G•d, and just lets it pass by.

his words."[68] "No fly passed over the table of the prophet Elisha."[69]

The Baal Shem Tov taught:

Wherever a person's thoughts are, so is he surrounded by spiritual worlds that mirror his thoughts. If his thoughts are holy, so is he surrounded by holy worlds, but if his thoughts are impure, so is he surrounded by impure worlds.

By the same token, wherever a person's thoughts are, and whichever worlds surround him, so is he surrounded in this earthly world, be it with kosher birds and animals, or non - kosher birds and animals.[70]

And there are three categories of worlds: the pure, the impure, and the in between. Above these categories is the world of pure thought, which cannot be fathomed.

---

[68] Tractate *Sukkah* 28a
[69] Tractate *Berachot* 10b
[70] In the source text (*Ben Porath Yoseph* 56d - 57a), the Baal Shem Tov adds that whatever happens to a person is also a mirror of his inner world. Thus, G•d is constantly talking to each and everyone of us, trying to make us aware of what is going on inside us. And hence, when we see some human act "out there" that is "non - kosher," we should look inside ourselves for similar failings, rather than judge the other person.

This, then, is why any bird straying above Rabbi Yonathan son of Uziel was burnt,[71] and why no fly passed over Elisha's table, by way of which his host knew that he was a holy man, because his thoughts were holy.

44. The Baal Shem Tov taught:

The letters of Torah study and prayer are the vehicles for dveikut/Oneness with G•d. One must concentrate one's thoughts and one's deepest being on the deepest spirituality that lies within the letters.[72] This is the deeper meaning of the verse, "May He kiss me with the kisses of His mouth,"[73]

---

[71]"Straying birds" is an allusion to straying thoughts, which were "burnt" by Rabbi Yonathan's Torah study. Similarly, no fly, being a non - kosher creature, flew over Elisha's table, because his thoughts were always holy.

[72] The Hebrew letters are actually symbols of the deepest spiritual secrets in Creation, and serve as conduits to transmit those spiritual energies into the world. All these different energies symbolized by the different letters ultimately all come from G•d, and are thus different expressions of the One. If one is able to enter deeply into a meditative state whereat the letters and the words that one is uttering are experienced as different expressions of the Divine wisdom and love that they indeed are, one then "unites" with G•d, as if with a kiss, since his human mouth uttering those words is then one with G•d's, so to speak.

[73] Song of Songs 1:2

which refers to the dveikut/union of souls,[74] as alluded to in the verse, "If you lie down between the lips."[75]

Thus, when one extends the pronunciation of a word, this is a sign that one has become one with it, since he does not want to leave that word.[76]

45. The Baal Shem Tov taught:

All letters of the aleph — beit are included in each individual letter. This is because the source of all letters is the Aleph, which is close to the

---

[74] *Zohar* II 124b. This refers to both the uniting of two human souls in this manner, and to the uniting of man's soul with G•d. The intense experience of union on the human level is a metaphor for the union of the human soul with G•d.

[75] Psalm 68:14. This verse is interpreted this way in the *Tikkunei Zohar*, quoted by Rabbi Moshe Cordevero, in his *Pardes Rimonim* 8:13.

[76] Rebbe Nachman of Breslov expounds on this idea and says that while one must continue from one word of prayer to the next, each word begs the one who expresses it to remain with it in *dveikut*. The solution, says Rebbe Nachman, is to make the entire prayer into "one," which means that the *dveikut* state achieved with each word be maintained throughout the prayers, so that even when has reached the last word, one is still with the first (*Likkutei Moharan* I 65:2). This state of consciousness can only be achieved when one has indeed reached a certain level of "Oneness," whereas one's mind and entire being are "at one" with G•d, and the individual letters and words are experienced as different manifestations of the One.

Oneness of the Infinite One.[77] Afterwards, the rest
of the letters expanded from the Aleph. For
instance, the Beit is really two Alephs, and so on,
until one reaches the Tav, which is equivalent to
four hundred Alephs. Thus, the letter Tav, the last
letter, is the furthest from the Creator.[78]

However, the tzaddik is able to gather all the
letters and return them to the Aleph,[79] and then
harsh judgment is sweetened at its source.[80]

---

[77] The *gematria* (numerical value) of the *Aleph* is one.
Although the Oneness of G•d is beyond "counting," that is,
G•d is not the "First" of a set, but the Absolute, Indivisible
and All - Encompassing One beyond any relationship to any
other entity, the letter *Aleph* represents the "closest" one can
get to G•d's Oneness. The metaphor provided here for this is
that just like the *Aleph* — the numerical value of one — is
included and "hidden" within all other numbers, since all
other numbers are really only composites of the number one,
so in everything that exists is "hidden" the Divine Oneness,
for everything that exists is made up of different "composites"
of that Oneness. Thus, by the same token, says the Baal
Shem Tov here, all letters are included in all others, since
essentially, underlying all letters is the One. In modern
terms, this phenomenon is called holography.
[78] The more complex and "multiple" one is, the further one is
from the Undifferentiated One. The way out of duality is to
experience the underlying Oneness, which is what the *tzaddik*
teaches us to do, as the Baal Shem Tov concludes.
[79] This idea is similar to the idea expressed by Rebbe
Nachman, quoted in the previous section.
[80] All harsh judgment is seen as only a result of duality and
division. When one is able to see through the apparent duality
of this world, as expressed by the duality of the numbers,
which themselves represent the duality of the world, and to

46. "The Jewish people were not exiled until they denied G•d and the dynasty of King David."[81]

"The only difference between the world at present and the world at the time of the Messiah is the subjugation to the [gentile] kingdoms."[82]

The Baal Shem Tov taught:

The Talmud teaches, "Whoever has not suffered for forty days has thereby received his future reward. And what is considered suffering? Even if one puts his hand into his pocket to take out a golden coin and instead takes out one of lesser value."[83]

However, since suffering is only in atonement for liability, how can such minor inconvenience constitute atonement?

The explanation is that since the righteous person lives with G•d, he believes in Divine providence and knows that G•d is guiding all events in his life down to the smallest minutiae, and that all his suffering is an expression of Divine justice —

---

perceive everything as unique expressions of G•d's Oneness and Design, all judgment automatically disappears.

[81] *Yalkut Shimoni*, I Samuel #106
[82] Tractate *Pesachim* 68a
[83] Tractate *Erchin* 16b

DINA, which is represented by the Divine Name of ADoNaI — on account of his sins.

Hence, as soon as the righteous person suffers however slightly, he immediately [searches his soul and] regrets [any misdoing], and becomes filled with anxiety and fear of G•d. He is thus immediately forgiven, since he believes [that his suffering is from G•d], and he repents and binds his mind to G•d.

Therefore, even when one is only slightly inconvenienced by having not taken out the coin he intended, since this only happened because of his sin, and he [is aware of this and] repents, this constitutes atonement.

This concept is referred to as "David" [made from the letters dalet, vav, dalet], for the Infinite One, Who is referred to as Ayin/Nothingness, is represented by the [first] dalet. "Nothingness" is then conveyed via the vav to the [second] dalet, which represents the nadir of nothingness, which is expressed by a belief that everything that happens is Divine providence from G•d.

However, when a person does not believe that everything that happens is Divine providence from G•d, but rather attributes things to his own actions, this is considered having denied G•d and the aforementioned concept of "David," for he is

denying the justice [providence] of the Kingdom of
G•d/ADoNaI.

But G•d's Kingdom is hidden and subservient
to the kelipot/shells that cover and conceal G•d's
providence from mankind.[84] In the future, though,
with the coming of the Messiah, who will banish the
spirit of impurity from the earth, G•d's providence
will be revealed even in the minutest of events.

With this we can understand, "The Jewish
people were not exiled until they denied G•d and
the dynasty of David," and, "The only difference
Between the world at present and the world at the
time of the Messiah is the subjugation to the
[gentile] kingdoms."

Understand this well,[85] for everything that a
person is able to comprehend about G•d is only
regarding His Malchut/Kingdom, but above that
cannot be comprehended.

---

[84] These "shells" are the "laws" of nature, the apparent cause -
and - effect, and in this case, the statistical but "chance
probabilities" that seem to govern whether one picks the gold
coin or the copper one from one's pocket.
[85] Until here is quoted from the *Toldot Yaakov Yoseph*,
VaYishlach #8. The conclusion is that of the compiler of the
Keser Shem Tov, and its relevance to the rest of the piece is
not clear.

47. The Baal Shem Tov taught:

Since the Jewish people had already said, "We will do and obey whatever G•d says,"[86] why does oral tradition say that G•d had to impose the Torah on the Jewish people by holding Mount Sinai over their heads and threatening to bury them underneath it if they didn't accept it?

The answer is that this comes to teach us that even when one has no desire to learn Torah and serve G•d, nevertheless, one is not absolved from doing so, and one must force oneself by visualizing that [G•d] is [now holding Mount Sinai over his head and] forcing him.[87]

51. "Although these [the academy of Shamai] forbid, and these [the academy of Hillel] permit, both opinions are the Words of the Living G•d."[88]

The Baal Shem Tov taught:

The different opinions are only in the lower worlds of duality, but in the upper world of Binah,

---

86 Exodus 24:7
87 This is not meant merely as a theoretical thought, but as a meditative visualization that can reignite the enthusiasm of, "We will do and obey," that naturally wanes and waxes throughout the day.
88 Tractates *Yevamot* 13b; *Eruvin* 13b

which is referred to as "the Living G•d," everything is Unity.[89]

51a. If G•d's presence fills the universe, if there is no place where He is absent, and if He can be found wherever a person is, then why are angels required to bring a person's prayers up to G•d from chamber to chamber?

The answer is that G•d arranged things this way so that it would seem to a person that he is extremely distant, and would strive to get closer.

This can be understood with the following parable the Baal Shem Tov.[90]

There was once a great and wise king who used optical illusions to give the impression that he had built walls, towers and gates around his palace. He then gave the order that whoever comes to him must go through the gates, and that treasures be scattered at all the gates. Thus, some people who came to see king found treasures at the first gate, took it and immediately turned around and went home, while others continued going

_____

[89] The *Toldot Yaakov Yoseph* in *VaYechi* #3 and in *Mishpatim* #9 quote this in the name of an anonymous sage, but in *VaYakhel* #3, the *Toldot* writes that he *thinks* he heard this from the Baal Shem Tov.
[90] *Ben Porath Yoseph* 111a

through more gates until they could not carry anymore treasures, at which point they too turned around and went home. However, the king's only son was not interested in the treasures, but only in reaching his father. He then realized that in reality, there were no walls at all separating him from his father, and that it was all an optical illusion.[91]

The analogy of the story is that G•d hides Himself in various veils and walls. However, His glory fills the universe, and every single movement or thought is only Him. Thus, even all the angels and heavenly chambers were all created from His very essence, like the shell of an insect is an integral part of its body. Hence, there is absolutely no separation between man and G•d, and with this knowledge, all evildoers are dispersed.

---

[91] This graphic parable portrays life as one great treasure hunt for the ultimate treasure – that of finding the One Who is hidden within all the little treasures and pleasures of life. The "treasures" at the gates are thus all the material and even spiritual pleasures that one can enjoy in this world, but none of these, on their own, can be considered "having found G•d," which is the goal of the entire scheme. G•d, indeed, created the world to afford pleasure to His creatures, but the ultimate treasure can be nothing else and nothing less than He Himself, and anything else and anything less is nothing but a decoy for the "Real Thing." The object of the game, though, is to find G•d hidden within all of those decoys, to reveal that, in essence, they are actually a part of the "Nothingness". . . .

55. The Baal Shem Tov taught:

Someone who performs a great mitzvah, learns a lot of Torah or prays with devotion should not allow thoughts of pride to enter his heart, as if he had done this. Rather, it was the Malchut [In dwelling of the Divine presence] — the ANI[92] from AdoNaI — that has done this. But when one prides oneself in having done this, he causes the letter yud[93] from ANI to disappear, and then only AN is left.[94] This is the meaning of, "Know from whence — from ayin — you come,"[95] literally, from nothingness, because when a person considers himself as nothing, then he comes close to G•d. On the other hand, when one prides oneself that one has done something, then one goes away from G•d

---

[92] *Ani* means, "I," and is the same letters as *ayin*, which means nothing. The implication of this is that each individual person's "I" is only a manifestation of the Divine "I," but to connect with this higher "I", we must transcend our lower "I," our egos, and realize that ultimately, we are *ayin*, we are nothing.

[93] The letter *yud* represents nothingness, since it is written as a single point of ink. It also represents wisdom. Living with a sense of our nothingness before G•d is true wisdom.

[94] Until here is a quote from the Baal Shem Tov in *Toldot Yaakov Yoseph, Korach* #3. Regarding the remainder, the *Toldot* in *Ben Porath Yoseph* 77a is not sure if he heard this too from the Baal Shem Tov, or if this is his own interpretation.

[95] Tractate *Avoth* 3:1

– the yud has disappeared, and only an remains. This is alluded to in the conclusion of the Mishnah, "To where — to an — you are going."

56. The Baal Shem Tov taught:

Wherever a person's thoughts are, that's where he fully is.[96]

63. The Baal Shem Tov taught:

There was once a king who had a son whom he wanted to teach many fields of wisdom. So he hired for him many wise men to teach him, but the prince was unsuccessful in learning any wisdom. Eventually, all the wise men despaired, and only one of them remained with him.

Once, the prince saw a beautiful young lady and desired her. The wise man rushed to warn the

---

[96] This thought was already expressed in #43 regarding the spiritual world in which a person is at any moment, or the physical world that surrounds a person at any given time. Perhaps this quote is adding that this is so not only regarding the surrounding physical world, but also regarding one's own physical body, and even if one is actually not "there." This is because thoughts are so potent and have such an effect on one's body, that the thought alone will create the virtual reality as if the body was indeed "there." An echo of this idea is found in the Sages' teaching that fantasizing about sinning is worse than the actual act, when one's mind may likely be somewhere else . . . .

king about this, but the king answered him, "If he does have desire, even though this be for something sensual, he will eventually attain all types of wisdom."

So the king ordered to bring the young lady into the royal courtyard, and commanded her to reject the prince's approaches unless he agreed to learn some field of wisdom. She did this, and kept telling him that he must learn another wisdom and another, until he had learned all fields of wisdom. By the time he had attained all this wisdom, though, he was not interested anymore in the young lady, because a princess was more fitting for him.[97]

---

[97] *Ben Porath Yoseph* 88a. Although the parable involves a wise man guiding the prince, a person can accomplish the same thing by "tricking" oneself and constantly postponing one's baser desires until one has made some spiritual attainment, after which one would postpone it again. Of course the prince did not realize that it was only a trick, whereas we would, but it is still possible to act "as if" one didn't know about the trick. This parable bears an echo of Rabbi Nachman's famous parable of the turkey prince (*Rabbi Nachman's Stories*, Breslov Research Institute, p. 479; *Under the Table*, BRI).

Another point in the story is that in the end, the prince does get married anyway, so what was gained? The answer is that while he was attracted to the first young lady simply on the physical level, by the time he acquired his wisdom, he realized that all earthly pleasures are really a distant reflection of the

This would explain why the Mishnah asks, "What is the difference Between Abraham's followers and Bilaam's followers,"[98] [after having delineated the good traits of these compared to the bad traits of those]. The intent is to differentiate between them even when Abraham's followers possess the same bad traits as the followers of Bilaam. Nevertheless, Abraham's followers will reap spiritual benefits from those traits both in this world and the next, as we see in the above parable, whereas Bilaam's followers will only spiritually deteriorate until they descend to hell.

64. The Baal Shem Tov said in the name of Rav Saadiah Gaon:

A person should learn a lesson from his desires for physical pleasures how he should desire to serve G•d and love Him.[99]

---

sublime spiritual pleasure of being with G•d, which is represented in this parable by his marrying the princess.

[98] Tractate *Avoth* 5:19

[99] This teaching is mentioned in *Ben Porath Yoseph* 88b in connection with the teaching of the previous section (#63). In this context, the prince in that parable sublimated and transformed his desire for the young lady into a desire for wisdom, and ultimately for G•d. Doing this, though, requires getting in touch with and experiencing that baser desire, for only then can one experience it as concealing a desire for G•d, and only then can one learn any lessons from it.

65. The Baal Shem Tov taught:

Dissolving one's being into one part of Oneness is tantamount to dissolving one's being into the entire Oneness.[100] The opposite is also true.[101]

66. "I searched for my soul's beloved, but I did not find him."[102]

G•d, the King of kings, conceals Himself within many different "garments," and behind many different walls. These include the thoughts that distract from Torah study and prayer, as the Zohar says, that the Light is surrounded by the darkness, as in the above parable of the King.[103]

---

[100] *Ben Porath Yoseph*, 88a. The metaphor given elsewhere for this is that of one grasping a branch of a tree. We would surely say that he is grasping the entire tree, for if he were to shake the branch, the entire tree would shake. And similarly, G•d, in His Unfathomable Oneness, created a world that reflects Himself, and is inherently an interconnected one, and anything affecting one part of the universe inevitably affects the entire universe. Hence, whenever one experiences a sense of oneness with any part of the universe, including of course with another human being, he is actually experiencing a sense of Oneness with G•d.

[101] That is, experiencing separation from any part of the Oneness is experiencing separation from the entire Oneness, for there is only one Oneness, and either one experiences Oneness or one does not.

[102] Song of Songs 3:2

[103] On the other hand, it is only because we live in the darkness, only because G•d conceals Himself, that we even

However, for knowledgeable people who know that there is no place absent of G•d's presence, such "concealments" are not concealments for them. This is alluded to in the verse, "Our leaders — our Aluph — are bearable,"[104] alluding that when we are aware that G•d — the Aluph/Leader of the world — is in all places and all situations, then all suffering is bearable.[105]

68. The Baal Shem Tov taught:

"What is the difference between the disciples of our forefather Abraham and the disciples of Bilaam?"[106]

The question here is obvious. The answer is that even the disciples of Abraham possess the trait of a proud spirit, and the opposite is also true, that the disciples of Bilaam possess the trait of a

---

search for the Light and seek to find G•d. This idea is included in the kabbalistic teaching that G•d's constricting the Light — the *tzimtzum* — was the greatest act of love on G•d's part, for without it, man would never have been able to find G•d.

[104] Psalms 144:14

[105] Rebbe Nachman of Breslov is quoted as saying, "When we lose our health, Who is taking it, if not G•d? When we lose a child, Who takes him, if not G•d?" (*Rabbi Nachman's Wisdom*, Breslov Research Institute, p. 335 - 336).

[106] Tractate *Avoth 5:19*. A different explanation of this Mishnah is presented in #63.

humble spirit. The only difference is that Bilaam's disciples use their traits in material matters, and Abraham's disciples use their traits in spiritual issues. That is, the disciples of Abraham elevate their hearts in G•d's service with their proud spirit and aspire to perform great deeds, while the disciples of Bilaam perceive themselves as unworthy with their humble spirit and absolve themselves from fulfilling G•d's will.[107]

69. "Avoid evil and do good."[108] This means avoid evil by transforming it into good.[109]

---

[107] The notion that we do not deserve to serve G•d is a spiritual obstacle for anyone who lives with awareness of G•d's greatness and man's comparative insignificance. The only way this notion can be overcome is by realizing that even the most awesome spiritual beings are insignificant before G•d, as is the awesomeness of the cosmos. Nevertheless, beyond all human comprehension and above all human rationale, the Infinite G•d chose the infinitesimal mortal man on this speck of dust Planet Earth to serve Him and perfect His creation. Experiencing this awareness is indeed simultaneously the epitome of humility and paradoxically the peak of pride, and is the point at which the human "I," *ani*, dissolves into the Divine "I," *Ani* (see #55).

[108] Psalms 34:15

[109] *Ben Porath Yoseph.* There are two ways of dealing with evil: overcoming it and subduing it, or transforming it, as said here. While the path of overcoming entails a constant struggle, and is based on the perception of inherent evil, the path of transformation entails a shift in perception, an awareness that all perceived evil is in reality only an illusion.

70. "G•d saw that [Moses] went to look, and He called out to him, 'Moses, Moses'."[110]

The Baal Shem Tov taught:[111]

Moses was initially concerned that this vision before him was not a holy vision, until G•d called out to him, "Moses, Moses." Only then did Moses respond, "Here I am."

For Moses' soul, as alluded to by his name, encompasses all worlds, which is why Moses could not comprehend his own name, as we shall see. For just as the Divine presence encompasses all worlds — the inanimate, the vegetable, the good and the evil — so does Moses' name: the first letter *mem*, which alludes to the Divine *Malchut*/presence, also encompasses all things, while the second letter *shin* encompasses all spirits, and the last letter *heh* encompasses all souls.

This idea is embedded in the parable of the king who created walls around him by the use of optical illusions, so that his son would eventually see through the illusion (#51), and in the parable in the *Zohar* of the king who hired a prostitute to entice his son. In practice, this means that instead of struggling with one's baser desires, one should elevate one's intentions while involved in actions usually motivated by one's baser desires.
[110] Exodus 3:4
[111] *Ben Porath Yoseph* 126c

Therefore, Moses' difficulty in comprehending the Menorah, the shekel, and the New Moon (HaChodesh), alludes to his difficulty in comprehending his own name (Moses = Mosheh), his own essence, since his name also encompassed good and evil. Furthermore, his difficulty was also in comprehending how the Divine presence Itself, the *Shechinah*, is the Ultimate Unity, since It encompasses the antitheses of good and evil, yet remains One Indivisible Unity. Thus, he was confused how he, whose name was Moses, which encompassed these antitheses, could bring about such Unity. Indeed, tradition records that Moses had the tendency to be a kidnapper/gambler.[112]

However, the truth is that evil is a vehicle for good, as we find in the teaching that Pharaoh

---

[112] Tractate *Berachot* 5a. The two alternatives are given by *Rashi* and *Tosafot*, respectively, and neither interpretation is very complementary. Furthermore, there is a Midrash in which a king versed in physiognomy requests to see a portrait of Moses, and upon seeing it remarks that this person possesses all the worst traits in the world. The point is that Moses grew to become Moses not only despite, but *because* he had to overcome the existential human inner conflict between good and evil tendencies. And the spiritual light that appeared with him at birth, as according to oral tradition, was not a manifestation of his inborn perfection, but of his *potential* to unify these dichotomous elements within his personality into and towards the singular goal of serving G•d, as in this teaching.

brought the Jewish people to repentance by pursuing them,[113] or by the fact that beholding the ways of the wicked brings a righteous person satisfaction and pleasure that he is not like that. This arousal of pleasure from contrast to evil exists in all worlds, and evil itself also has a virtual elevation from this, only that when good rises in this way, all evil is dissolved in the process.[114] And in the same way, all evil thoughts can be vehicles of elevation.[115]

Thus, Moses did not answer G•d after the first call of his name, since he did not comprehend how Unity could be achieved, for when the lowest spiritual levels were revealed, as symbolized by the bush, all their higher spiritual sources were also revealed to him. Therefore, Moses could not understand why evil — as represented by the bush — was not "burnt" by those sublime spiritual levels. Then G•d called out to him again, "Moses," alluding that the Ultimate Unity is achieved specifically by the union of the lowest levels with the highest. Only then did Moses say, "Here I am."[116]

---

[113] *Zohar* I 81b.
[114] Psalms 92:10
[115] This idea is alluded to in #69 and expounded upon in #39.
[116] As mentioned in n. 109 in #69, there are two ways of dealing with evil: subduing it or transforming it. When Moses

71. The Baal Shem Tov taught:[117]

When one feels that one's service of G•d is not going well, one should acknowledge that the appropriate verse at this time is, "I [G•d] have sworn in My wrath/*Aph* [that they will not enter My peaceful Sanctuary]."[118]

For even during a period of Divine wrath — *Aph* — one must realize that this is only a manifestation of the eight lower *Sephirot*[119] below

---

first saw the fire of the burning bush, he understood the fire to symbolize that the bush, representing evil, as said in the text, must be "burnt," and subdued. But then he saw that the fire was not consuming the bush — which he understood to mean that all efforts to vanquish evil are doomed to fail. If so, he thought, that evil is an existential reality, does this not point to Duality, to an existence outside of G•d? But then G•d called out to him a second time, "Moses," thereby alluding to him that he, too, was a seeming duality — a "lower" and an "upper" Moses: a very human Moses with all human frailties and weaknesses, but also a "G•dly" Moses, and both were parts of his unique singularity. Then Moses realized that the fire in the bush was not symbolizing destructive power of fire, but its "light" — the potential of transformation. Then Moses realized that both evil and good are really part of the One. Then Moses answered, "Here I am" — an integrated one.

[117] *Ben Porath Yoseph* 126c
[118] Psalms 95:11
[119] The letters *aph* inverted are the Hebrew letter *Phe*, which is numerically equivalent to 80, a integer of 8, representing the eight lower *Sephirot*, each of which is a complete holographic system of the ten *Sephirot*, as is known.

Binah,[120] and that even in the *Aph* – the *Phe* – is hidden the letter *Aleph*, representing the *Aluph*/Leader of the World. In this way, one sweetens[121] the *Aph*, the Divine wrath.

72. The Baal Shem Tov taught:[122]

Regarding thoughts, there are many different types of thoughts, some good, some evil. But even within falsehood there is truth, for the numerical value of falsehood — *SheKeR* — is 600, which is inclusive of truth — *Emet* — the numerical value of which is 441.[123]

---

[120] *Binah* is the lower of the two upper *Sephirot* connected with knowledge and understanding, while in comparison, the eight lower *Sephirot* as a whole are connected with a lack of understanding and with constrictions, which give rise to such periods of Divine wrath. The implication here is that one must bring this higher understanding — this experiential reality — into one's period of constricted consciousness.
[121] The use of the metaphor, "sweetening" the judgments, used so extensively in Chassidic texts, alludes that what is "done" does not change the essence of the *Aph*, but only makes it palatable to us, just as sweetener makes food palatable. This fits in with the idea of the previous two teachings (#69 and #70), that all evil is only from our perspective, and we transform evil by transforming our awareness, and recognizing it as concealed Divine love.
[122] *Ben Porath Yoseph* 126c
[123] This teaching is found in the quoted source immediately after the teaching of #71, and continues the same idea. All evil and falsehood conceals within it the good and the true, as alluded to by the numerical values — the numerical value of

73. The Baal Shem Tov told this parable:[124]

There was a king who had three servants. Once, a rumor reached the king that they were not loyal to him, so he ordered that each of them should choose one of the dogs in the royal courtyard and feed and support it.

One of the servants was wise, and made a crown for the king with the money that could have gone to support his dog. The second servant only fed his dog enough that it shouldn't die. The third servant, though, fed his dog very well.[125]

---

evil (280) is also greater than of good (17), the large difference perhaps implying that good is frequently extremely hidden within evil, whereas falsehood must contain a large amount of truth in order for it to be accepted.

[124] *Ben Porath Yoseph* 126d

[125] This parable is a metaphor for G•d's intention regarding the evil inclination, similar to the metaphor in the *Zohar* of the king who hired a prostitute to entice his son. Here, the king wants to test the loyalty of his servants, so he orders them to feed a dog — the evil inclination. The king's intention, of course, was not that they really feed the dog, which the wise servant understood. So this servant takes the money that he would have put into the dog and puts it into glorifying the king. By the same token, our task is to take the energy that we could put into fulfilling our evil inclinations and transform it into glorifying G•d. We "crown" G•d when we are able to see through the veil of evil and to recognize how G•d is hidden even there. We have then coronate G•d over all corners of existence. This is the path of transformation spoken about in #69. The second servant, though, followed the path of overcoming and subduing — he virtually starved the dog, a method of mortification once commonly used to overcome the

The king provoked the dog to attack the third servant, but not the one who made him a crown.[126]

77. "Warm yourself before the fire of the sages, but be careful not to burn yourself from their coals, for their bite is like the bite of a fox and their sting is like the sting of a scorpion, and all their words are like burning coals."[127]

The Baal Shem Tov taught:

Before beginning study, the sages used to make light conversation[128], in order to open their minds from a constricted state of *katnut*/immature consciousness and bring themselves to an expanded state of *gadlut*/mature consciousness.

For there are constricted and expanded states in the dimensions of world, time, and soul. When the world is in a state of expanded consciousness,

---

evil inclination. The third servant, of course, is the one who fulfills his desires and evil inclinations, and thus only increases their hold on him, as represented by the king provoking the dog.

[126] The parable only speaks about the king's response to the first and third servants, but the second servant seems to be ignored. Indeed, as said in the previous note, the second servant represents the one who tries to serve G•d, but his path is not what G•d really desires.

[127] Tractate *Avoth* 2:10

[128] Tractate *Sabbath* 30b

one can come close to G•d very easily, whereas when the world is in a state of constricted consciousness, then one has to struggle tremendously in order to come close to G•d. However, the greatest spiritual benefits are reaped when one has to force oneself to serve G•d.

Thus, even when one is unable to immerse oneself in strictly spiritual practices, one should nevertheless bind G•d's Word in his heart,[129] even while busy with mundane chores. When the sages spoke in praise of Torah study together with mundane endeavors, they were speaking specifically about this.[130]

Hence, when a student comes to learn before his master when the master is in a state of constricted consciousness, he might observe the master involved in mundane chores and learn only that from him, not realizing that his behavior is then only like a coal, without any inner fire.[131] For

---

[129] Psalms 119:11

[130] Tractate *Avoth* 2:2. The nuance of meaning in the *Mishnah* is that Torah study and mundane endeavors should be pursued simultaneously, which can only be done in the way presented here, where one retains consciousness of G•d's Word while busy with mundane chores.

[131] The metaphor of a coal is used because the fire inside the coal is not evident. Similarly, the spiritual ember inside the heart of the master is not visible on the outside.

this reason, the *Mishnah* warns, "Be careful not to burn yourself from their coals."

This is also alluded to in conclusion of the *Mishnah*, "Their sting like the sting of a scorpion." In Hebrew, a scorpion is an *AKRaV — Ayin KaRaV* — meaning, the sage is involved in bringing the seventy [*ayin*] dimensions of the mundane world[132] closer [*karav*] to their Source, but this student does not realize this, and assumes that the master's mind is only on the mundane.

78. "What is the onus for slaughtering? One opinion says for coloring, and another opinion says for taking life. [The opinion that says for coloring means for coloring and *not* for taking life? No, he means also for coloring."[133]

The Baal Shem Tov taught:[134]

We are taught that the evil inclination will be brought to justice in the Future. The question is, how can it be held responsible for doing what it was

---

[132] The letter *ayin*, numerically seventy, represents the spectrum of the ten *Sephirot* in each of the seven lower *Sephirot*, which in general are connected with the mundane world, as opposed to the upper three, which are generally connected with the world of thought and above.
[133] Tractate *Sabbath* 75a - 75b
[134] *Ben Porath Yoseph* 127a

created to do? The answer is, it will be brought to account for disguising itself as the good inclination.[135]

This is alluded to in the above teaching, "What is the onus for slaughtering?" This refers to the evil inclination that slaughters man's soul. Why is it held responsible, since this is what he was created to do? The answer is, because it "colors" itself and disguises as the good inclination, and is thus able to trick man and take his soul.

This is also alluded to in the verse, "The words of his mouth are evil and deceit;"[136] evil refers to sin, and deceit refers to fooling man into believing he is doing a good deed. As a result, as the verse concludes, "He refrains from understanding to improve;" man does not repent from his "sins," because he believes them to be good deeds, and one does not repent from doing good deeds.

---

[135] If the average person would be confronted by something about which he was absolutely sure was improper conduct that he could not justify to himself, let alone to others, he would not have the temptation to do it. So the evil inclination fools man into rationalizing away his negative behavior, denying its true nature, and perceiving it as impeccable conduct with the noblest motivations.

[136] Psalms 36:4

79. "He thinks evil on his bed, he stands on a path that is not good."[137]

This refers to someone who prays in his illness — "on his bed" — fooled by the evil inclination into asking G•d's assistance in merit of his good deeds, when in truth, "he stand on a path that is not good."[138]

80. The Baal Shem Tov taught:

The most important thing when praying in exile is faith — to believe that G•d's glory fills the earth. By so doing, one elevates and exalts the *Shechinah*/Divine presence.

One must also believe that as soon as one expresses the words of prayer from his mouth, his request is answered. And even when one's request does not seem to be answered, this is because the answer has remained hidden from him. For example, his request may have been answered for the benefit of the world in general, although he had

---

[137] Psalms 36:5. This verse follows the one quoted at the end of the previous teaching, and is explained as continuing the same idea.
[138] Not only is a person fooled into acting improperly and justifying himself by believing that he acted properly, but he then turns around and expects G•d to assist him in merit of that "good deed."

requested that his personal suffering be removed. However, this itself is for his benefit, for instance, to atone for his sins. But if the intention of one's request is that he personally should be answered, then one has entered an element of [materiality] into his request. One's request should be solely for spiritual benefit, for the sake of the Shechinah/Divine presence, and not for some earthly benefit, which creates a veil of separation.[139]

This, then, is the meaning of, "Jacob lifted his legs"[140] — which refers to the "legs" of the Shechinah/Divine presence[141] — by virtue of his

---

[139] The teaching begins with a statement that G•d's glory exists equally throughout the earth, an axiom that itself is an aspect of Oneness. Acknowledging this is in prayer reveals the Divine presence *to the one praying* — it "elevates and exalts the Shechinah." But for this to be revealed to the one praying, for one to experience the Oneness, one cannot have one's personal needs in mind, because this creates a "separation" between oneself and the Oneness. One must rather perceive oneself as an inseparable part of the totality of the Oneness of creation, and pray for the benefit of that Oneness, for one automatically benefits from the benefit of the Oneness. This is the meaning of "praying for the sake of the Shechinah," because G•d's presence is revealed on earth, as said, only to the extent that man perceives the Oneness of creation.

[140] Genesis 29:1

[141] The "legs" of the Shechinah are a reference to the lowest spiritual levels, just as the legs are the lowest part of the body (*Degel Machaneh Ephraim, VaYaytzay*). Jacob was able to

faith and trust, as the verse says, "Take courage and strengthen your hearts, all those who trust in G•d."[142]   And this is the meaning of the oral teaching on the verse, "Jacob lifted," which says that his heart lifted his feet after he was promised [that G•d was with him].[143]

81. The Baal Shem Tov taught:

If all suffering and other issues for which one should pray will disappear with the times of the Messiah, what will happen to prayer itself? — for we can surely not say that prayer itself, which is considered a "limb of the *Shechinah*/Divine presence,"[144] will be abolished. Furthermore, the verse says, "On that day, the iniquity of Israel will be sought but there will be none, and the sin of

---

elevate the people at these levels because of his faith that G•d can be found within their worlds as well, in other words, that he, at his exalted spiritual level, and they, at their lowly levels, are equally part of the singular body of mankind in general, and the Jewish people in specific.

[142] Psalms 31:25

[143] Rashi *ad loc.* Since Jacob was promised that G•d was with him, by automatic extension, He is with Jacob's "feet," the lowest levels. This encouraged Jacob to indeed elevate those levels with this very message.

[144] *Zohar* I 10b (where the metaphor is actually wings).

Judah but not found."[145] Why will they be sought?
Who will need the iniquities of Israel?

The answer is that there are four categories of
suffering that evoke prayer. The first is when one is
pained by the desecration of G•d's Name among the
nations, and prays for this. The second is [when
one is pained] for having sinned, for the greatest
suffering is sin. Sin, in fact, is even worse than
death, for while death atones for sin, sin causes
many types of death. The third is prayer for one's
sustenance, and the fourth is for life itself.[146]

Now, the "limbs of the Shechinah/Divine
presence" are enwrapped within the four categories
of suffering just mentioned, so that one should be
moved to pray, while seeing through the veil of
those superficial circumstances and elevating the
Divine sparks hidden within them.[147]   However,

---

[145] Jeremiah 50:20

[146] These four categories seem in an order of descending
levels, from the most spiritual to the most physical. One who
prays for the desecration of G•d's Name is not praying for any
personal salvation, but rather of that of mankind and the
entire universe. Praying for having sinned, however sincerely,
involves a personal salvation.

[147] When one prays with an awareness that one is indeed
talking to G•d, he experiences himself being in G•d's
presence. At that moment, one has indeed "revealed" G•d in
the world – in his world. G•d was always there, but we did
not see Him. So G•d puts us through painful experiences so
that we call out to Him from our suffering, so that perhaps we

when one is not confronted by one of those four painful circumstances, one does not realize that one should pray.[148]

This, then, is the meaning of the verse, "The iniquity of Israel will be sought," so that it could be prayed for, but there will be none, or "The sin of Judah" – the Hebrew word "sin" means a lack, in this case, the lack present in any of those painful circumstances — "but it will not be found." Thus, on that day there will be nothing to pray for, and prayer will then be only to make unifications.[149]

---

may come to realize that the suffering was only a means to bring us to Him. Nevertheless, when one has indeed reached this level of prayer at which one is "at Oneness" with G•d, the prayer itself has becomes transformed from a means to the goal. This may be alluded to in the metaphor of "limbs." On the one hand, limbs are not actually part of the main part of the body — the head and torso — but only extensions that serve it, to bring things to the body or to bring the body somewhere. On the other hand, though, the limbs are certainly part of the totality of the body, and the entire body can be seen as one entity.

[148] Regarding this, Rebbe Nachman of Breslov said that one should train oneself to speak to G•d about everything that is going on in one's life, as if one were talking to one's best friend.

[149] Until here is from the *Toldot Yaakov Yoseph, VaYikra* 2, and the remainder is an addition of the compiler. As said, the goal of prayer is to attain Unification with G•d, for which suffering is only a means. But when mankind will reach this level, suffering will no longer be needed as a means, and prayer will then be to reach ever higher levels of Unity.

For all physical acts that are done in this world are all alluded to in the Torah, and are all included in the World of *Atzilut*/Closeness as stated in the *Zohar*. The main thing, though, is to believe beyond any doubt that the words of prayer bring about the immediate reality of that for which one is praying.[150]

This also explains the verse, "Jacob sent messengers to Esau."[151] Jacob [Ya'AKoV] represents the *Shechinah*, for the first letter *yud* is the raw potential[152] that becomes enclothed in the seven levels of material existence, which are represented by the second letter *'ayin*,[153] each of which is inclusive of the ten levels of existence, each of which are inclusive of the ten *Sephirot*, which are represented by the third letter *kuf*.[154] All this is accomplished by way of *Binah*, which is represented by the fourth letter *beit*, which refers to

---

[150] This idea was already presented in the previous piece (#80).

[151] Genesis 32:4

[152] The letter *yud* is "raw potential," because it is only a dot of ink, from which all other letters can be drawn.

[153] The letter *'ayin* is numerically 70, composed of the seven levels times ten levels.

[154] The letter *kuf* is numerically 100.

he two "angels"[155] that were sent "to Esau," to the world of *Asiyah*/Action.[156]

82. The Baal Shem Tov taught:

When a person transgresses one sin, he will be confronted with the test of another sin, so that he became aroused to repent, whereby the first sin will be atoned. When the evil inclination sees this, it tries to overpower the person with this second sin, but [even if he succumbs,] G•d defends him, as the verse says, "For three sins of Israel [I can forgive them]."[157]

---

[155] The letter *beyt* is numerically two. In the writings of the Rabbi Yitzhak Luria, the two Supernal *Sephirot* of *Chokhmah* and *Binah* are referred to as "angels" (*Pri Etz Chaim, Shabbat* ch. 20).

[156] The physical world, represented by the lower seven *Sephirot*, are "mindless" and "chaotic." Each function seeks its own fulfillment, and does not interact with another. This creates our world of apparent separateness. However, by bringing Mind into play – the Mind of the two higher *Sephirot*, *Chokhmah* and *Binah*, the dissonance of the different *Sephirot* are transformed into the harmony of a single orchestra, all interacting harmoniously to produce something beautiful. This is an aspect of the Oneness and Unity that one must strive to achieve in one's personal life, and for the world at large.

[157] Amos 2:6. The Talmud in Tractate *Yoma* 86b uses this verse as the basis of the statement that G•d does not punish for a person's first two sins (see Maimonides, *Teshuvah* 3:5, *Keseph Mishneh ad loc.*). With a third sin, though, one has already entrapped oneself within the force of habit, and his

However, after a person has already sinned three times, the three levels of his soul — his *nefesh, ruach* and *neshamah*[158] — are caught up in the *klipot*,[159] and one sin then inevitably brings another in its wake, and the paths of repentance are withheld from him, until G•d has mercy on him.

And this is what the prophet means, "Let us search our paths and analyze them, and return to G•d,"[160] for after one's path has become a trodden way in one's eyes, because "the heart of this people has become thick,"[161] one must search and analyze one's behavior in order to realize that one has sinned.[162] Only then will one return to G•d.

---

repentance then becomes very difficult, as we read in the next paragraph. One is thus held responsible for all successive sins, although they may well be considered being done under the force of compulsion.

[158] From here we see that with every repetition of a physical act, the influence of that act seeps deeper and deeper into one's soul.

[159] Someone "caught in the *klipot*" — the "shells" or "husks" — does not even realize that he is trapped. Just as shells and husks conceal what is inside them, so do the *klipot* prevent one from seeing oneself clearly and objectively.

[160] Lamentations 3:40

[161] Isaiah 6:10

[162] It is not easy to change a habit, but even more than this, once one has become accustomed to certain behavior, one tends to rationalize it and justify it, thus making it difficult to even admit that the habit *needs* changing. Only honest soul searching introspection can see through this self-deception.

83. "Each day conveys an utterance, and each night expresses knowledge."[163]

The Baal Shem Tov taught:

Man's initial judgment is for abstaining from Torah study.[164] But a person assumes that he will be able to absolve himself from judgment because he was busy earning a living by day and resting from his toil by night. However, the short winter days prove him wrong, and the short summer nights contradict him.[165]

85. "'I, G•d, have not changed,' but G•d has changed in relation to the wicked, and has become hidden behind many veils and coverings. And this is the meaning of the verse, 'I will hide My face from them.' "[166]

---

[163] Psalms 19:3
[164] Oral tradition (Tractate *Kiddushin* 40b) derives this from a verse in Proverbs 17:14.
[165] Until the advent of electricity, the workday basically ended at sunset, and thus during the winter, people worked less hours. This proves that one is willing to work less hours when necessary, which raises the question, Why not for Torah study? Similarly, one sleeps less during the short summer nights, which shows that one is able to be flexible with one's sleeping hours, which contradicts the contention that one must rest the entire night.
[166] *Tikkunei Zohar* #26, 71b

From *them* G•d hides His face, but for those who stand in awe before G•d and His presence, He never changes. And though there are many different veils behind which G•d hides Himself, the Baal Shem Tov says that when a person realizes that G•d is hiding there, He is not hidden anymore, for all evil then disappears.

This then is the meaning of the verse, "I will hide My face" [the verb is repeated] — G•d will hide the fact that He is hidden.

And this is also the allusion in the verse, "The enemy said, 'I will pursue and overtake, and split [the booty]"[167] [the first five words of the Hebrew verse all begin with the letter *aleph*]: This alludes to the "five *Aleph*s,"[168] which alludes to the *Aluph*/Master of the world, as alluded to in the Divine Name *SaEL*,[169] which is numerically equivalent to the Divine Names of YHVH and ADoNaI together.

After a person realizes this rule, which is a major rule that states that there is absolutely no

---

[167] Exodus 15:9
[168] The five corresponds to the five levels of existence.
[169] This Divine Name is the source of the archangel, Samael, who is identified as the evil inclination and the angel of death, and everything associated with them. This alludes that even this angel is really only a veil behind which G•d hides Himself.

barrier between a person and G•d while he is praying or studying. And even if unwanted thoughts arise in his mind, they are only coverings and veils behind which G•d is hiding, once one realizes that G•d is hiding there, He is not hidden anymore.[170]

86. The Baal Shem Tov taught:

It is known that the Hebrew letter *aleph* represents wisdom and thought, as the verse alludes.[171] With this we can understand the first verse in the Torah, *"Breishit bara Elokim,"* which the Targum renders, "G•d created with *'reishith,'* with wisdom," which is the letter Aleph. Hence, G•d created the world with the letter *aleph.*

For all of the twenty - two letters of the *aleph - beit* are "garments" for one another. For example, the *aleph* is hidden within the *beit*, because *beit* is numerically two – two *alephs*, each of which is numerically one. Similarly, the *gimel* is three *aleph*s.

Thus, the initial stage of creation was with the letter aleph, which represents wisdom, meaning that everything was created with wisdom, as the

_____

[170] *Toldot Yaakov Yoseph, Breishit #1*
[171] Job 33:33

verse indeed says, "You created everything with wisdom."172 Hence, the spirit of G•d was enclothed within the *aleph*, with which G•d created the light – the *ohr* [which begins with the letter aleph], which is the Light of the World of *Atzilut* [which begins with an *aleph*]. After that, the spirit of G•d in the letter *aleph* became enclothed within the letter *beit*, with which G•d created the World of *Beriah*.173

87. The Baal Shem Tov taught:

"Sweetening the harsh judgments at their source," spoken about in the writings of the *Ari z'l*, is accomplished by a transmutation of letters, for any decree is only letters. This is the deeper meaning of Noah being instructed to make a window — a *tzohar* — in the ark: he was supposed to mitigate the harsh judgments into mercy by transmuting the letters of misfortune — *tzarah* — to *tzohar*.174

This is also alluded to in the verse, "When you go out to war against an enemy [in Hebrew,

---

172 Psalms 104:24
173 *Toldot Yaakov Yoseph, Breishith* #1
174 Furthermore, the Hebrew word for ark can also mean a word, thus the verse would be explicitly saying, Make the word into *tzohar*!

ha'tzar] . . . sound a stacatto on the trumpets."[175]
For the sound of a stacatto arouses joy, the
opposite of the sound of the *shofar*, which arouses
fear. This means that by accepting the pangs of
battles with joy, the suffering — *tzarah* — is
transformed into Divine grace — *ratzah.*

This is accomplished by binding the harsh
judgments connected with *Malchut* to *Binah*,[176] or
by finding within the harsh judgments some
element of kindness to which the judgment can be
attributed. Then, the harsh judgment is mitigated
at its source in kindness, and is revealed to be
indeed kindness.[177]

88. The Baal Shem Tov taught:

Every human being is composed of the Ten
Sephirot, since every human being is a microcosm
of Creation, and whatever is present in the
dimension of "world," is present in the dimensions

---

[175] Numbers 10:9
[176] *Malchut* is connected with a state of "not knowing," as
Malchut is referred to as "having no eyes," while *Binah* is
connected with a state of understanding. Hence, when one is
able to transcend one's not knowing, to submit one's human
understanding to that of G•d, one is able to mitigate the harsh
judgments by accepting them as being G•d's "better
judgment," even if one does not understand it.
[177] *Toldot Yaakov Yoseph*, Noah #3

of time and soul,[178] as alluded to in the verse, "Mount Sinai was full of smoke/*ASHaN*."[179]

The lowest level in man is connected with pain and suffering, and corresponds to the *Sephirah* of *Malchut*, as the verse [alluding to *Malchut*] says, "Her feet descend to death."[180] The *Sephirot* of *Netzach* and *Hod* are paralleled in man by the pillars of faith upon which he stands, which establish one's firm faith in G•d. The *Sephirah* of *Yesod* represents one finding more pleasure in serving G•d than from any other pleasure.[181]

---

[178] From here, and from the next paragraph, we see that this lesson is speaking about the human soul, and not the human body. The *Sephirot* are certainly represented in the human body, but that is included in the dimension of "world." Also, the specific "sites" of the *Sephirot* within their traditional depiction are also paralleled in the human body, as we also see from the next paragraph, with lowest *Sephirah*, the *Malchut*, represented by the bottom of the feet, the *Netzach* and *Hod* represented by the legs, and the *Yesod* represented by the organs of pleasure.

[179] This Hebrew word is an acronym of world (*aolam*), time (*shanah*), and soul (*nephesh*). The reason why these three levels of existence are alluded to with the word smoke is because G•d reveals Himself through these three channels, which are in fact veils — "smoke screens" — that conceal G•d as well as manifest Him (*Mei HaShiloach VaYaytzay, V'hineh*).

[180] Proverbs 5:5

[181] *Toldot Yaakov Yoseph, Lech Lecha* #4

89. The Baal Shem Tov taught:

If a person happens to witness or hear about someone having sinned, one should realize that there is some element of that sin within oneself, and should see to correct it.[182]

The verse provides us with guidance for this: "Guard your tongue from evil, veer evil and do good."[183] By so doing, even the sinner will repent, after one has included him within oneself by way of Oneness, since all mankind is one being. One thus "does good," and transforms the evil into good.

90. After a person experiences a period of spiritual elevation, one must return and descend in order to elevate those still on lower levels,[184] as alluded to in

---

[182] The underlying basis for this idea is presented in #43, where we learn that a person's external reality is only a mirror of one's inner world.

[183] Psalms 34:14. The implication here is that one should not judge that other person and spread gossip about him, but rather look inward. By honest self —introspection, one will find a similar evil within oneself, which is why the scene or the story was revealed to one in the first place. Then, one will be able to identify with that other person on that level, and by tapping in to that level at which they are one, one's own repentance will influence the other person to repent as well.

[184] This idea is connected with the previous teaching (#89), in that one can elevate others only by identifying and becoming "one" with them on some level. During periods of spiritual ascent, when one is experiencing a spiritual "high," one may

the verse, "I have washed my feet."[185] This is also the meaning of, "running and returning,"[186] and what is referred to as, "*katnut*/immaturity and *gadlut*/maturity."[187]

And every time one descends, one must take care to be able to rise again,[188] so that one does not remain in spiritual descent. For as the Baal Shem Tov said, many people fell and remained there.[189]

92. The phenomenon of "running and returning" exists in the physical world as well. This is alluded

---

tend to disassociate from those people still on lower levels, and is thus unable to elevate them. But when one has fallen oneself, one understands and identifies with the difficulty others are experiencing, and is thus able to elevate them with his own return.

[185] Song of Songs 5:3. The "feet" are a metaphor for the lowest spiritual levels, and the verse thus alludes to the thought that may go through the mind of someone presently at a higher level: I have "washed" my own "feet" already, so I don't want to dirty myself again.

[186] Ezekiel 1:14. This verse refers to the angels running towards and returning away from G•d, and is metaphor for the spiritual ups and downs of the human soul.

[187] Although physiological maturity is irreversible, spiritual maturity is cyclical.

[188] Although one may be in a state of spiritual descent, one must remain *aware* of this and not allow oneself to wallow in this state or to act in ways that would reinforce it.

[189] *Toldot Yaakov Yoseph, VaYera* #1. Indeed, the higher one goes, the deeper the potential fall, and the disappointment and frustration one experiences.

to in the Mishnah, "Make yourself warm near the fire of the wise."[190] This implies not to try and warm oneself from too far, but at the same time, not to come too close, until one is at the flame, as the Mishnah concludes, "Be careful from their coals, lest you be burnt."[191]

94. The Baal Shem Tov taught:

One should bind one's thoughts to the Light of the *Eyn Sof*/Infinite One that is within the letters, which is the life—giving "Light that is in the King's presence."[192] This is a major rule for Torah study and prayer, and is also remedy to annul harsh judgments.[193]

---

[190] Tractate *Avoth* 2:10
[191] *Toldot Yaakov Yoseph, VaYera* #2. As the *Toldot* explains there, when one "runs" toward G•d, one's being becomes "dissolved" and "absorbed" into His Oneness. Thus one loses one's own identity and in a sense, "nullifies" one's very existence. But this is not G•d's wish, but rather that a world continue to exist in *apparent* separateness from Him, so one must "return" to earthly existence and serve G•d from the "distance." Similarly, if one gets too "close" to the wise, one may tend to lose one's own identity by being overwhelmed by their spiritual light, and not grow to become what one is meant to become. One must thus find the golden median between submission to the wise and self - actualization.
[192] Proverbs 16:15
[193] When one studies G•d's Word in the Torah, or communicates with Him in prayer, one should aim to see through the individual ideas, words, and even letters one is

95. "When rain is withheld, one should seek out the most pious person in the generation, so that he prays. If he prays and is answered and becomes haughty, he arouses G•d's anger upon the world, as the verse says, 'He attains anger for haughtiness.'"[194]

The Baal Shem Tov taught:

If the pious person sinned by becoming haughty, what has the world done that it should suffer?

The answer is, that the ideal situation should be that, "He who ordained that oil should burn can also ordain that vinegar should burn," just as indeed happened for the saintly Rabbi Chanina son of Dosa.[195] If all people lived by the standards of

---

expressing, and behold the Oneness of the Infinite G•d that is hidden behind them. Everything ultimately arises from this Oneness, and when one reaches this, one has arrived at the very goal of Torah study and prayer. And since everything G•d does is for the best, when one reaches this level one realizes that there is no such thing as harsh judgments (*cf.* #33,85).

[194] Job 36:33; Tractate *Taanit* 8a

[195] Tractate *Taanit* 25a. The only reason why oil burns is because G•d so decreed in the laws of nature, but there is no inherent reason why He cannot ordain vinegar to burn. Therefore, pious people who live with the reality that all of Nature is G•d's constant miracles are able to evoke changes in the laws of Nature, because to them, it is all the same.

piety, no one would see it as extraordinary if one person was able to burn vinegar like oil simply by praying for it to burn, for everyone would be able to do this. However, since most people follow their frivolous ways, and only one pious person in a generation is able to do this, it seems extraordinary when that person's prayer is answered. Therefore, if a haughty thought arises in that person's mind, this is because of the people of the generation and the world. Therefore, anger is aroused upon the world.

97. "A prayer of the poor man when he beseeches, pouring out his words before G•d."[196]

The Baal Shem Tov explained with a parable:

A king once proclaimed on a day of his rejoicing that any request presented on that day would be filled. So some people requested positions of power, others requested honor, while others requested wealth, and each person was given what he requested. There was one sage there, though, who said that his request was to have a personal audience with the king three times a day.[197] The

---

[196] Psalms 102:1
[197] This of course alludes to the three daily Silent Prayers, the *Shmoneh Esreh*.

king was very pleased with this, since it showed that speaking with the king was more cherished by him than wealth and honor.[198] Thus, the king ordered to have his request fulfilled, to give him permission to enter the royal palace to speak to the king, and then to open the royal treasuries for him to also take wealth and honor. This is alluded to in the above verse: the prayer of a poor man is that he be able to pour out his words before G•d.

98. One should always praise G•d before praying.[199] One should always pray before praising G•d.[200]

The Baal Shem Tov taught:

These two Talmudic sayings do not contradict, but both are actually expressing the same idea.

The power of the Creator is in the Creation, and the world can be compared to the shell of an insect that is an integral part of its body. Thus, a

---

[198] As we saw elsewhere (#81), the purpose of prayer is to reach a state of Oneness with G•d, and the release from suffering for which we pray, or the benefits that we seek, are only the catalysts for us to pray and reach that goal. The wise man thus goes straight for the goal, by way of which he anyway attains relief and benefit.
[199] Tractate *Berachot* 32a
[200] Tractate *Avodah Zarah* 7b

spark of G•d can be found in all types of physical or spiritual pain, albeit hidden within a veil. This is alluded to in the verse, "The seven maidservants fitting to be given to [Esther] from the royal palace."[201]

Thus, when one deeply understands that G•d is with him right there and then, the veil is removed and all suffering ceases. This is what the first teaching means by saying that one should first praise G•d, because G•d's praise is that His Glory fills all the earth, and that He can be found amidst all pain. When one realizes this, the suffering ceases, as said, and one can pray, because the suffering will automatically cease, since one knows how to praise G•d in this manner.

The other opinion, though, says that one should pray first, that is, by believing that G•d is with him wherever he is, and then one is able to express G•d's praises.[202]

105. The Baal Shem Tov taught:

There are two types of wicked Jews: one acts only in privacy, while the other acts in public.[203]

---

[201] Esther 2:9
[202] *Toldot Yaakov Yoseph, VaYechi* #1
[203] From the context in which this piece appears in the source (*Toldot Yaakov Yoseph, Bo* #2), "wicked" in this instance does

The difference between them can be seen from the verse, "I saw an evil tyrant . . . . then he vanished, and behold — he was no more! So I searched for him, but he was not to be found" (Psalms 37:35,36). But why should one search for a wicked person who has vanished? The answer is because someone even more evil than he will take his place, which is why the previous one will be sought.[204]

106. "Pharaoh brought close."[205]

The Baal Shem Tov taught:

---

not mean sinning, but Jews who betray their people and try to harm them. The one who acts in public is not ashamed of his behavior, and is thus likely to be more dangerous than the one who is still uncomfortable about acting in public.

[204] The lesson of this teaching may be that one should never complain about one's situation, because it could always be worse. Indeed, Rebbe Nachman of Breslov said that if one complains, then G•d says that He will show that person what bad really is. On the other hand, if one praises G•d for one's situation, whatever it might be, G•d says that He will show him what good really is (*Siach Sarfei Kodesh* II [Breslov] p. 11, #32).

[205] Exodus 14:10. The sages comment that this verse implies that Pharaoh brought something else close. This, they say, alludes that Pharoah's chasing the Israelites brought *them* close to G•d, because they cried out to Him and repented. The Baal Shem Tov's teaching here is based on this comment.

When evil serves as a catalyst for good, then the evil becomes a vehicle for the good, and everything becomes completely good. This is virtually a complete nullification of evil, as will take place in the future. Deep concepts are contained in this idea regarding untoward thoughts, but let this suffice.

Similarly, when the sages said that Abraham's slave, Eliezer, was transformed from cursed to blessed because of what he did for Abraham, they were also alluding to this idea.

107. The Baal Shem Tov taught:

The reason why giving the body pleasure on the Sabbath is a *mitzvah* is because the spirit is then able to rejoice even more in being with G•d.

This can be understood with the parable of a captive prince who received a letter from his father.[206]

---

[206] *Toldot Yaakov Yoseph*, *Bo*, #8. The entire parable is found in the *Toldot* in *Kedoshim* #1: A king's only son was taken captive. After many years, during which much effort and hope was put into redeeming him and returning him to his father, the prince received a letter from his father, the king. It urged him not to become discouraged and not to forget the ways of royalty, despite living all these years among human wolves, for his father was still doing his utmost to bring him home by whatever means, whether by attacking or peacefully.

"When all these things happen to you – the blessing and the curse – then you will take it to heart ... and return to G•d."[207]

The Baal Shem Tov taught:[208]

We can understand why one would repent in response to suffering, but why does the verse mention also blessing?

This can be explained with a parable:

There was once a peasant who rebelled against the king, striking and stoning the king's statue. Upon hearing this, the king immediately appointed him to a position in his government, and continued to elevate him higher and higher, until the peasant became the viceroy. But the more the king treated him nicely and elevated him to a

---

The son was immediately extremely happy, but since this was a secret message, he could not rejoice openly. What did he do? He went to the local pub and drank with others, but while they were reveling in their liquor, he was rejoicing in his father's letter (see also other sources in the *Sefer Baal Shem Tov, Beresheit.*

The prince is the human soul, which is in "captivity" in the earthly body. Every week, the king sends the prince a letter of encouragement — the Sabbath. The body, though, is not interested in rejoicing in this spiritual message, and even scorns it, and must be "seduced" into rejoicing by providing it with in its own pleasures, so that the soul can then rise unfettered, in *its* ecstasy.

[207] Deuteronomy 30:1
[208] *Toldot Yaakov Yoseph, Bo #11*

higher position, and the more he witnessed the dignity of the king and the royal palace, the more this peasant was pained when he remembered how he had rebelled against this great and benevolent king, and that rather than punishing him justly, the king is treating him graciously.

But the king acted this way intentionally, for had the king simply put the peasant to death, the peasant would have suffered momentary pain and no more. This way, though, the peasant lives in constant pain for the rest of his life, and his pain increases each time the king elevates him, by ca using the peasant to beat himself over how he ever dared to rebel against such dignity.

This parable is alluded to in the verse, "G•d is a G•d of vengeance. G•d of vengeance reveal Yourself!"[209] G•d exacts vengeance by way of His mercy,[210] unlike the norm for a human king. This is accomplished when G•d reveals His greatness to someone, who is then pained by realizing how he has rebelled against such a great King. What greater pain can there be?

This, then, is the meaning of returning to G•d in response to "the blessing and the curse." When

---

[209] Psalms 94:1
[210] This is alluded to by the fact that the Divine Name of mercy is used in this verse.

a person sins and rebels against G•d — the Great and Awesome King, the Master and Controller, the Root and Source of all worlds — that person deserves to be punished severely. But instead, G•d grants him blessing. There can be no greater curse or suffering than this, from his knowing that he rebelled against G•d, Who only graciously blesses him with good. This person will certainly weep bitterly in pain for the rest of his life for his having rebelled against G•d.[211]

And this pain, which is greater than any punishment could exact, is itself the atonement.

109. The Baal Shem Tov taught:[212]

Someone who tries to run away from pain and distress, but they follow him wherever he goes, is like a birthing woman who tries to escape from

---

[211] Reality, though, seems to contradict this, because the most fortunate and materially blessed people in the world are rarely the most righteous, and in fact, sometimes quite to the contrary. This is because these people do not acknowledge that their blessing comes from G•d, and they have no inkling of G•d's greatness. Indeed, the *Toldot* (*ibid.*) concludes that this teaching only applies to an understanding person, but when the spiritual fool sees that he can act against G•d's Will without forfeiting his bounty, he thinks that either his bounty does not come from G•d, or that there is no difference to G•d between the saint and the sinner.

[212] *Toldot Yaakov Yoseph, Beshalach* #4

her labor pains by going somewhere else, but the pains follow her. The only way is to pray to G•d, and only that will get rid of the pain.

This is the meaning of the verse, "I called G•d in distress; G•d answered me with relief."[213]

This is also the meaning of the verse, "Egypt was pursuing them," upon which the Israelites realized their situation and, "The Israelites called out to G•d."[214] Indeed, right afterwards the verse says, "As you have seen the Egyptians today, you will never see them again."[215]

---

[213] Psalms 118:5

[214] Exodus 14:10

[215] *Ibid.* v. 13. The *Sefer Baal Shem Tov* on that verse quotes a teaching of the Baal Shem Tov that renders the verse to be saying, "*Because* you saw the Egyptians today, you will never see them again." That teaching is obviously based on the one here. But the question is, how can we say that the escape from distress - from Egypt - was in response to the Israelites' prayer, when the intermediary verses there relay their complaining to Moses? The answer is, that on a deeper level, this teaching is based upon another one, that as soon as one realizes that one's distress comes from G•d, all suffering disappears, although not necessarily the painful situation itself. Thus, the Israelites were still confronted with what seemed like a dead end, about which they only humanly complained, despite their having accepted their fate as coming from G•d. But *because* they had acknowledged their "Egypt" — their distress (the Hebrew letters are identical) — as coming from G•d, there was no longer any need for them to be confronted with it, and they therefore never had to see it again.

APPENDIX

GLOSSARY

Achiyah HaShiloni — The Heavenly teacher of the Baal Shem Tov. In prior incarnations, Achiyah HaShaloni witnessed the exodus from Egypt, was a prophet during the time of King David, and taught Elijah the Prophet.

Amidah — (lit. standing as it is a prayer that is to be recited inaudible in a standing position); also referred to as the Shemonah Esreh (eighteen benedictions); the main section of daily prayer, recited standing and inaudibly.

Arizal — acronym for Eloki Rabbi Yitzchak — the Divinely inspired Rabbi Yitzchak Luria (1535 — 1572) — whose teachings became central for virtually all Kabbalistic thought thereafter.

Asiyah — (lit. deed); The final level in the Divine creative process which includes the physical universe.

Atzilus — (lit. emanation); The realm of spiritual existence which, although encompassing attributes which have a specific definition, is in a state of infinity and at one with the Infinite Divine Light.

Beriyah — (lit. creation); The realm of spiritual existence which represents the first beginnings of a consciousness of self.

Binah — (lit. comprehension); The stage of the intellectual process that develops abstract conception, giving it breadth and depth.

Barchu — (lit. bless); One of the responsive readings in congregational prayer.

Chassid — (lit. pious one); One who observes beyond the letter of the law; A follower of the Chassidic movement (pl. Chassidim).

Chazan — (lit. cantor); One who leads the congregation in prayer.

Cheder — (lit. room); A Torah school for young children.

Chesed — (lit. kindness); The Divine attribute of benevolence.

GLOSSARY

Chochmah — (lit. wisdom); The stage of the intellectual process for abstract conception.

Daat — (lit. knowledge); The third stage of the intellectual process at which concepts, having proceeded from seminal intuition through meditative gestation, now mature into their corresponding dispositions or attributes of character.

Dinim — Divine judgments.

Dveikus — (lit. clinging); A profound concentration and spiritual attachment.

Gadlut — (lit. greatness); The expanded state of consciousness and existence.

Gevurah — (lit. might); The attribute of restraint, associated with the restriction of Divine emanation.

Hod — (lit. splendor); One of the Divine attributes.

Kabbalah — (lit. received tradition); The body of Jewish mystical teachings.

Katnut — (lit. smallness); The constricted and narrow state of consciousness and existence.

Kedusha — (lit. holiness); A passage in the public prayer service with portions recited responsively by the chazan and congregation.

Kelipot — (lit. shells); The outer coverings which conceal Divinity within all creation; hence, the unholy side of the universe.

Kriyat Shema — The recitation of the daily declaration of faith, recited in the morning and evening prayers, as well as before retiring to sleep.

Machzor — The prayer book used specifically for the High Holidays.

Malchut — (lit. kingship); The Divine attribute of might or power.

Midot — Divine and mortal attributes of character, spiritual emotions, and mental states.

Minyan — (lit. number); The quorum of ten necessary for communal prayer.

Mitzvah — (lit. commandment); One of the 613 commandments found in the Torah; a generally good deed.

Mochin — (lit. brains); The three attributes or stages of the intellectual process.

Moshiach — (lit. the anointed one); The Messiah.

Ne'ilah — (lit. closing); The fifth and final prayer service recited on Yom Kippur.

Netzach — (lit. victory); The Divine attribute of eternity.

Penimiyut — (lit. innerness); The endeavor to make one's deeds and attainments an integral part of one's being; the opposite of superficiality.

Pesukei D'Zimrah — (lit. verses of praise); The selection of passages which appear early in the morning prayer service and lead into the declaration of faith.

Ramban — Rabbi Moshe ben Nachman, also known as Nachmanides (1194 -1270).

Rosh Hashanah — (lit. head of the year); The solemn New Year holiday.

Satan — The Accusing Angel.

Sefirah — One of the Divine attributes or emanations which are the source of the corresponding faculties of the soul.

Shabbat — (lit. rest); The Sabbath, the Divinely — ordained day of rest on the seventh day of the week.

Shamash — (lit. attendant); The synagogue beadle.

Shechinah — The Divine Presence.

Shefah — The flow of Divine life force into creation.

Shema — The daily declaration of faith recited in the morning and evening prayers, as well as before retiring to sleep.

Shochet — (lit. ritual slaughterer); One who slaughters and inspects cattle and fowl in the ritually prescribed manner for kosher consumption

Tiferet — (lit. beauty); The Divine attribute of compassion.

Tzaddik — A wholly righteous person (pl. tzaddikim).

Yesod — (lit. foundation); One of the Divine attributes.

Yetzirah — (lit. formation); The realm of spiritual existence in which the limited nature of the created beings takes on form and definition.

Yom Kippur — The Day of Atonement.

Zeir Anpin — (lit. "small countenance); The collection of Divine attributes excluding Malchut (might).

BIBLIOGRAPHY

1. BAAL SHEM TOV FAITH LOVE AND JOY Vol. I
   by Tzvi Meir Cohn
2. BAAL SHEM TOV DIVINE LIGHT Vol. II
   by Tzvi Meir Cohn
3. BAAL SHEM TOV HEART OF PRAYER DIVINE
   LIGHT Vol. III
   by Tzvi Meir Cohn
4. IN PRAISE OF THE BAAL SHEM TOV
   Translated and edited by Dan Ben Amos and
   Jerome R. Mintz
5. THE PATH OF THE BAAL SHEM TOV
   by Rabbi David Sears
6. ESSENTIAL PAPERS ON CHASSIDISM
   Edited by Gershon David Hundert
7. THE LIGHT BEYOND
   by Rabbi Aryeh Kaplan
8. TZAVA'AT HARIVASH
   by Rabbi Jacob Immanuel Schochet
9. THE LIGHT AND FIRE OF THE BAAL SHEM
   TOV
   by Maggid Yitzhak Buxbaum

10. THE BESHT
    by Professor Emanuel Etkes
11. THE GREAT MISSION
    by Rabbi Eli Friedman
12. CHASSIDIC MASTERS
    by Rabbi Aryeh Kaplan
13. THE RELIGIOUS THOUGHT OF CHASSIDIM
    by Rabbi Norman Lamm
14. CHASSIDIC MASTERS
    by Rabbi Aryeh Kaplan
15. THE RELIGIOUS THOUGHT OF CHASSIDIM
    by Rabbi Norman Lamm

WWW.MEZUZAH.NET

Home of the World Wide Mezuzah Campaign

The fundamental goal of the World Wide Mezuzah Campaign is to unify the Jewish people. By fulfilling the mitzvah of Mezuzah, this unity can be accomplished by each Jewish person: man, woman or child. The mitzvah can be easily fulfilled by affixing a Mezuzah on the "Doorpost of Your House or upon Your Gates," as required by Jewish law.

Purchase Mezuzahs written in Israel by a Certified Scribe, then checked by a computer for accuracy and finally checked by a second Certified Scribe before we send it to you. Our Mezuzahs are of a very high quality, and they are beautifully written. They are shipped to you in a Mezuzah case ready to mount on your door.

www.mezuzah.net
The World Wide Mezuzah Campaign
A project of the Baal Shem Tov Foundation
A 501(c) (3), nonprofit organization

Baal Shem Tov Times

Spreading the light of the legendary
Kabbalah Master and Mystic

Rabbi Yisrael Baal Shem Tov

—A weekly email publication—

Regular Features:

Baal Shem Tov Story
Torah Baal Shem Tov
Heart of Prayer
Divine Light
Kesser Shem Tov

Subscribe to receive your FREE weekly
e-mail edition at
www.baalshemtov.com

About the Author

Yehoshua Starrett studied in yeshivot in New York, and later in Jerusalem, where he was introduced to the teachings of Rebbe Nachman and his followers, and to the world of Chassidic teachings in general. He is the author of The Breslov Haggadah, Esther: A Breslov Commentary on the Megillah, The Inner Temple, To Heal the Soul, which includes the spiritual journal of Rebbe Kalonymus of Piasezna, Peace Talks: Greeting Your Fellow Human Being in Jewish Law and Practice, and the following works in progress: The Breslov Bencher (grace after meals), Chanukah: Breslov Teachings, and a rabbinical commentary on the Bible.

ALSO PUBLISHED BY BST PRESS

BAAL SHEM TOV FAITH LOVE AND JOY Vol. I

BAAL SHEM TOV DIVINE LIGHT Vol. II

BAAL SHEM TOV HEART OF PRAYER Vol. III

BAAL SHEM TOV GENESIS Vol. I

BAAL SHEM TOV EXODUS Vol. I

BAAL SHEM TOV LEVITICUS Vol. III

BAAL SHEM TOV NUMBERS Vol. IV

BAAL SHEM TOV DEUTERONOMY Vol. V

BAAL SHEM TOV HOLY DAYS Vol. VI

BAAL SHEM TOV GENESIS EXODUS Vol. I

BAAL SHEM TOV LEVITICUS NUMBERS
DEUTERONOMY Vol. II

Printed in Great Britain
by Amazon.co.uk, Ltd.,
Marston Gate.